ECE/TIM/DP/26

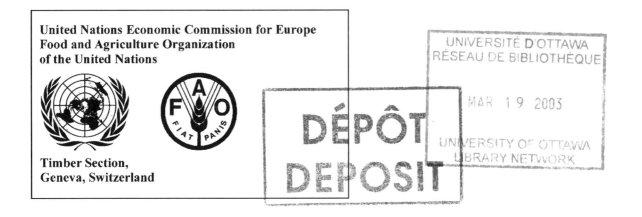

Geneva Timber and Forest Discussion Papers

FOREST AND FOREST PRODUCTS
COUNTRY PROFILE

GEORGIA

Prepared by Ms. Kate Metreveli

Forest Development Project

UNITED NATIONS

New York and Geneva, 2002

Note

The designations employed and the presentation of material in this publication do not imply the expression of any opinion whatsoever on the part of the secretariat of the United Nations concerning the legal status of any country, territory, city or area, or of its authorities, or concerning the delimitation of its frontiers or boundaries.

Abstract

This *Forest and Forest Products Country Profile,* prepared by the national expert, contains information concerning the forest resources of Georgia and a description of the status, trends and developments taking place in the forest sector and of the areas in which forestry activities have taken place over the past decade. For the forest sector, as for other branches of the Georgian economy, the period has been marked by the implementation of radical reforms necessitated by the changeover from a centrally planned to a market economy and by efforts to achieve sustainable development in forest management. The country profile contains tables, statistical data, diagrams, graphs and a brief analysis of the evolution of the forest sector, and data relating to the principal categories and volumes of goods and services in the forestry sector. Most of the figures cited are based on official data drawn from the statistical services of Georgia, as well as from research and statistics from NGOs and other foreign sources. Detailed information will be found in the annexes, which contain information on the social and economic situation of Georgia, as well as forest resources and forest products (import/export) data.

ECE/TIM/DP/26

UN2

E/ECE/TIM/DP/26

UNITED NATIONS PUBLICATION
Sales No. E.03.II.E.19
ISBN 92-1-116833-3 ISSN 1020-7228

UNECE/FAO TIMBER AND FOREST DISCUSSION PAPERS

The objective of the Discussion Papers is to make available to a wider audience work carried out, usually by national experts, in the course of ECE/FAO activities. They do not represent the final official output of the activity, but rather a contribution which because of its subject matter, or quality, or for other reasons, deserves to be disseminated more widely than the restricted official circles from whose work it emerged, or which is not suitable (e.g. because of technical content, narrow focus, specialized audience) for distribution as UNECE/FAO official documents.

In all cases, the author(s) of the Discussion Paper are identified, and the paper is solely their responsibility. The designation employed and the presentation of material in this publication do not imply the expression of any opinion whatsoever on the part of the secretariat of the United Nations concerning the legal status of any country, territory, city or area, or of its authorities, or concerning the delimitation of its frontiers or boundaries. The ECE Timber Committee, the FAO European Forestry Commission, the governments of the authors' country and the FAO/ECE secretariat, are neither responsible for the opinions expressed, nor the facts presented, nor the conclusions and recommendations in the Discussion Paper.

In the interests of economy, Forest and Forest Product Country Profiles are issued, without final languages editing. They are available on request from the secretariat. They are distributed automatically to nominated forestry libraries and information centres in member countries. It is the intention to include this Discussion Paper on the Timber Committee website at: http//www.unece.org/trade/timber. Those interested in receiving these Discussion Papers on the continuing basis should contact the secretariat.

Another objective of the Discussion Papers is to stimulate dialogue and contacts among specialists. Comments or questions should be sent to the secretariat, who will transmit them to the author(s).

PREFACE

The UNECE Timber Committee and FAO European Forestry Commission, working in close co-operation on the sustainable forest management, pay special attention to those regions and member countries, which are not always in the mainstream of the global forest policy debate. One efficient way of drawing attention to specifics of the forestry sectors of such countries is the preparation of forest and forest products sector country profiles.

The sector profiles are prepared in consultation with national experts and include statistical and other information. The objective of the current forestry profile on Georgia is to show the role and the importance of forests and forestry in this Caucasian country against the background of the country's current economic and social situation.

With one of the lowest levels of real GDP per capita in the ECE region, Georgia is highly dependent on the supply of resources and energy, including wood/timber resources. Georgia possesses forest ecosystems that are extremely rich in biodiversity. The transition to a market economy has revealed many issues in the forestry sector, which made it necessary to carry out urgent reforms to start economically, ecologically and socially sound forest management.

For this reason Georgia had to develop a new forest policy that would guarantee the protection of the forests' ecological, protective, and social functions, while at the same time providing the country with responsibly produced wood to improve the economy. The new forest code, which laid a foundation for both institutional and policy reforms in the forestry sector was adopted in 1999.

The sector profile was prepared by Ms. Kate Metreveli, who was working on the Forest Development Project in Georgia. We would like to express our gratitude to the author for the excellent work.

Mr. Hosny El-Lakany
Assistant Director-General, FAO
Forestry Department

Mrs. Brigita Schmögnerova
Executive Secretary
UN Economic Commission for Europe

Symbols and Abbreviations

AR	Autonomous Republic
DPA	State Department for Protected Areas
FAO	United Nations Food and Agricultural Organization
GEL	Georgian lari (currency)
GDP	gross domestic product
ha	Hectare
IDSS	Institute of Demographic and Social Studies
IMF	International Monetary Fund
m.a.s.l.	meter above the Sea level
MOE	Ministry of Environment
NEAP	National Environmental Action Plan
NGO	Non-governmental Organizations
ob	over bark
SFD	State Forestry Department
sob	solid over bark
TACIS	Technical Assistance to the Commonwealth of Independent States

TABLE OF CONTENTS

A – Demographic Situation in Georgia

B – Social-Economic Situation

C – Data of Forest Fund

D – Wood Utilization

E – Actual and Planned Forestry Activities

F – Non-wood Products

G – Import / Export

H – Institutions

Introduction

The Country Profile includes the overall picture of the history and present day of Georgia (one of the former Soviet Republics that is undergoing a critical transition) along with the statistical data, brief analysis and outlook of the Georgian forestry sector (including the forest resources, industry, production, trade and prices of forest products). There is also a list of relevant official organizations. Due to the fact that the data presented in this profile are based not only on official statistics, but also on outcomes of research carried out by foreign experts and NGOs, the accuracy of some information may be open to discussion, but it is considered to be the best available.

Brief Historical Sketch

Georgia, known to Greeks and Romans as Kolkheti (western part of the country) and Iberia (eastern part), adopted Christianity in the IV century under the influence of Byzantium. The country managed to unite during the X-XIII centuries despite numerous invasions by Arabians, Mongolians, Turks and Persians. This period in Georgian history is called "Golden Era". Recollections of this period helped preserve a national self-awareness in the following centuries, when foreigners conquered Georgia. Russia, which started annexation of this region in 1801 and finished it in 1917, was the last among such conquerors. Georgia was integrated into the Soviet Union in 1921, but it became an independent Soviet Republic of the Soviet Union in 1936.

Georgia is an independent, unified and indivisible law based state. This was ratified by the referendum carried out on March 31, 1991 throughout all the territory of the country, which consists of 63 administrative districts. The population of the country was 5.5 millions in 1989. The political order of the Republic of Georgia is a democratic Republic. The territory of Georgia occupies 69.7 thousand square kilometers.

The Georgians are an ancient people, whose long history has been marked by intensive interactions with other nations and cultures, such as Assyria, Urartu, Greece, Rome, Parthia, Arabia, Byzantium, Mongolia, Iran, Turkey, Russia and the Western European countries. Through more than 30 centuries of such interactions, Georgians have managed to preserve their unique language, culture, and identity. The Georgian state counts its history from the 12th century BC. Due to its productive land and strategic location astride the crossroads between Europe and Asia, Georgia has always attracted the attention of traders as well as potential conquerors. Ancestors of the Georgians practiced nimble diplomatic skills, seeking to maintain good relations with their neighbours, but sometimes bloodshed was unavoidable.

Some time in the 4th century BC, the Georgian alphabet was created. The oldest surviving text in the Georgian language is dated to the 5th century AD. In the 4th century AD (particularly in 337 in the Kartli region) Christianity was accepted as the state religion.

Georgia's power and influence reached their peak during 11th-12th centuries. Mongolian invasions, which began in the 13th century, significantly weakened the Georgian state. Georgian Monarchs sought help from Western European countries and the Pope, but the western Europeans and Papacy were preoccupied with crusades, and thus unable to assist. With the rise of the Turk-Osman Empire on Georgia's western borders, and the Turks' conquest of Constantinople in 1453, Georgia was geographically isolated from Western Europe and the Christian world as a whole. As part of its effort to re-establish ties with other Christian nations, Georgia eventually established diplomatic relations with Russia. In 1801 Russia abolished the Kartl-Kakhetian kingdom and formally incorporated it into the Russian empire. Not long thereafter, an independence movement started in Georgia. It was on 26 May 1918 that Georgia gained its independence, and started to move towards rebuilding and development, but in 1921 Soviet Russia annexed Georgia.

Even after the forced integration into the USSR, Georgians managed to preserve their national identity and never complied to subjugation. After the collapse of the USSR in 1991, Georgia again started to rebuild its statehood. The road to development was paved with bloody conflicts and civil wars, but the country retained its vision to ensure equality of all its citizens through the new constitution, free and fair elections, and the establishment of local democracy. The 1990s in Georgia were characterized by sharp political and social-economic changes, followed by demographic crisis. As of 1997, the total population in Georgia was estimated to be roughly 4.4 million inhabitants (although, if Abkhazia and Former South Ossetia are excluded this number would be approximately 4.2 million). The last population census in Georgia was held in 1989 (which is the basis for the 1990-97 estimates), which showed a population of 5.4 million inhabitants. Results of the ongoing population census are not finalized yet. The permanent population according to the 1989 population census (5400.8 thousands) was taken as a base for the 1990-97 calculations.

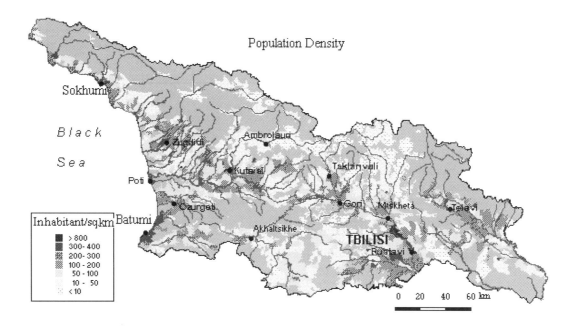

Population Density

Table 1
Population 1990-97
(1,000 people)

	1 January*		Average annual*		1 January**	Average annual**
	1	*2*	*3*	*4*		
1990	5456.1	5456.1	5460.1	5460.1	5421.7	5437.30
1991	5464.2	5464.2	5463.5	5463.5	5452.9	5457.85
1992	5462.8	5462.8	5454.9	5454.9	5462.8	5313.40
1993	5447.1	5447.1	5440.3	4874.5	5164.0	4925.50
1994	5433.5	4867.7	5425.6	4859.8	4687.0	4593.25
1995	5417.7	4851.9	5416.9	4851.1	4499.5	4420.75
1996	5416.0	4850.2	5419.8	4859.7	4342.0	4276.85
1997	5423.6	4869.1			4211.7	

Note:

1.   Population of Georgia including Abkhazia AR and Ossetian AR;

2.   Population of Georgia excluding Abkhazia AR and Ossetian AR, commenced 1994;

3.   Average annual population of Georgia excluding Abkhazia AR and Ossetian AR, Population commenced 1993;

4.   Population of Georgia excluding Abkhazia AR and Ossetian AR, commenced 1994 (respectively 1994 and 1993).

Source:*State Statistics Department data; **Institute of Demography and Federal Research of Academy of Georgia.

Graph 1
Population Dynamics

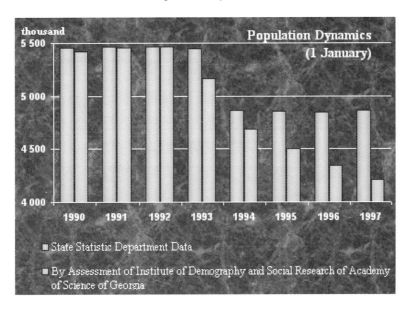

In the official statistical data of 1994-96, the population of Abkhazian AR and former South Ossetian AR (565.8 thousand inhabitants) are excluded from the total of Georgia. In 1997 this number was equal to 554,500 people. From 1993 on, official data on population does not take into account 200,000 refugees. Nevertheless, this data is significantly different from the number calculated by the IDSS, which is extrapolated via different methods. As of 1997, the difference between these two numbers is 657,000 people, thus the demographic indicators are different.

Table 2
External Migration of Population of Georgia, 1990-96
(1,000 people)

Year	Official Statistics			Statistics by IDSS		
	Immigration	*Emigration*	*Balance*	*Immigration*	*Emigration*	*Balance*
1990	20.0	59.0	-39.0	27.2	42.9	-15.7
1991	16.6	60.6	-44.0	20.9	49.5	-28.6
1992	8.0	49.6	-41.6	50.0	305.0	-225.0
1993	12.6	42.9	-30.3	74.0	264.0	-190.0
1994	12.7	44.2	-31.5	79.0	277.0	-198.0
1995	3.7	23.9	-20.2	70.0	246.0	-176.0
1996	1.2	12.9	-11.7	57.0	200.0	-143.0
1990-96	73.8	292.1	-218.3	378.1	1384.4	-1006.3

Source: State Statistics Department; IDSS

By the calculations of the IDSS, at this period, more than one million citizens were outside of Georgia. This data is quite different from the official data because the official source of information takes into account only permanently migrating persons, while other source (especially IDSS) records illegal external migrations as well as temporary travels outside the country.

Graph 2
Migration of Population

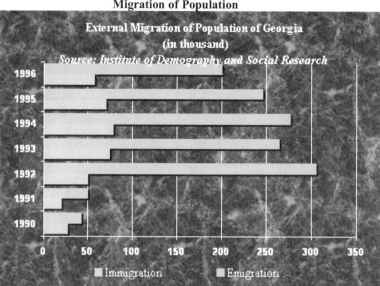

Source: Institute of Demography and Social Research

The population of Georgia consists of more than 100 nationalities. The main population in Georgia consists of Georgians (70 %) The capital of Georgia is Tbilisi. (population over 1.3 million people) The state language in Georgia is Georgian, but in Abkhazia, Abkhazian is also the state language. The state recognizes the special importance of the Georgian Orthodox Church in Georgian history, but simultaneously announces complete freedom in religious belief and the independence of the church from the state.

General Social – Economic Situation

Before independence, the Georgian economy was one of the strongest in the USSR. It revolved around Black Sea tourism, cultivation of citrus fruits, tea and grapes; mining of manganese and copper, and the output of a small industrial sector, producing wine, metals, machinery, chemicals and textiles. The country imported the bulk of its energy needs, including natural gas and oil products at a subsidized rate from other parts of the Soviet Union. Its internal energy resource, hydro-electricity, generates 80% of Georgia's electricity needs. A chronic lack of power resources remains a serious problem.

While Georgia was part of the former Soviet Union, it ranked 4th in standard of living (after the Baltic Republics). After the collapse of the Soviet Union, Georgian industrial and agricultural production lost its sales market. The economic infrastructure was nearly destroyed during the period of 1992-1995 because of civil war, ethnic conflict, and criminality, throwing Georgia into a deep depression. As a result of this situation, the flow of foreign investments into the country was also severely hindered.

Georgia's economy, already reeling from the loss of Soviet subsidies after independence, was severely damaged by the Abkhazia and South Ossetia civil conflicts. Hyperinflation in the early 1990s reached 7,000% per year by 1994, and by 1995, Georgia's gross domestic product (GDP) had fallen to 20% of 1990 levels. Since then, however, GDP has levelled off and a recovery has begun, with the help of the International Monetary Fund (IMF) and the World Bank. Georgia's currency, the Lari, was introduced in September 1995 and has remained relatively stable with the backing of an IMF stabilization fund. Inflation, estimated at 4.6% in 2000, has been brought under control, and GDP growth has resumed, although it has been moderated (1.9% in 2000) by the lingering negative effects of Russia's August 1998 financial crisis.

Introduction of a national currency significantly revived the consumer market and gave stimulus to economic restoration. Nowadays, the Georgian economy is rapidly developing (by 1997 the rate of increase was 14%). Despite the current trend toward growth in the economy, there are a number of problems; industrial production is small while imports are high (80-85% of consumption). The unemployment rate is also high (according to preliminary estimates, 20-25% of the capable population). As a result, the standard of living and gross domestic product per capita are very low; credits and grants received from donors still form the main part of income to the country's budget.

History of Forestry in Georgia

The history of forestry in Georgia can be divided into three time periods: before the Soviet Union (until 1921), during the Soviet Union (1921-1991), and after Georgia's declaration of independence (after 1991). In old Georgia, forest use was free. The cutting of trees for fuel wood, construction material, or clearing the land for other forms of land use (grazing and cultivation) was often seen as harmful, even in historical documents, which mention such positions as " chief forester" and " forester" whose duty it was to manage and protect the forests. Later according to the law, "water, wood and grass" belonged to the state and it was no longer permitted to use them free of charge. In 1801 Georgia was annexed to Russia. In the beginning, the forests were managed as before, in an uncontrolled manner with no consideration for reforestation. While people made use of the forest as they saw fit, without any consideration for public good, the low population and the fact that the country was 60-65% forested, helped to mitigate the damage. Timber trading (and attempts to get paid for forest use) developed during the 1830s with large amounts of wood, mainly species like oak, walnut (*Juglans regia*), chestnut (*Castanea sativa*) and box wood (*Buxus colchica*) exported to Turkey, Egypt, France and other countries, but the internal timber trade was still small.

Forest management in Georgia was first implemented in the Borjomi forests where the first forest inventory was carried out in 1854. From 1810 to 1870, Georgian press and intelligentsia debated the merits of organized forestry, paid forest use and protection of the forests. According to specialists of this time, some 105,000-110,000 ha of forestland had been changed into agricultural use, and large quantities of young trees were cut for poles needed in the wine industry.

In the 19th century, before the Soviet period, the forests belonged to the state, private landowners, churches and monasteries and also to villages (which typically belonged to individual families, but were in common use).During the 1864-1871 period, peasant reform was carried out, freeing the serfs, but still protecting feudal interests. According to the rules of the time, peasants were able to buy forestlands (which proved very difficult as most had little resources to buy forest or agricultural land). For this reason few peasants became forest owners.

During the period of 1885 to 1917, the forest cover in Georgia was reduced to 654,113 ha. In 1921, all the forests were declared to be state property, and forest management, including forest inventory, protection and reforestation was started. The agricultural public commissariat was put in charge of the forests. As per the new forestry legislation, in 1923 the forests were divided into two groups, general state forest and local forests. That same year, resort forests were handed over to the Health Care public commissariat. In 1928 the Georgian public Commission's Council declared eleven forest districts state parks many of which are still functioning.

With the improvement of the economy, followed the process of national industrialization and a need for great resources, including wood. The pressure on the forest resource increased rapidly. In the period of collectivisation, very large area of lowland forest were felled and the land taken over by tea, citrus, grape, and by collective farms. The timber processing industry developed noticeably from 1926-27. The forest was divided into industrial forestry and cultural forestry zones under the Soviet Union regulations of 1931. Under the central directives, all the forests of Georgia, with the exception of the resort forests, were united into a group of "industrial forests under the central directives, in spite of their need for very careful management. This was a disaster for the forests.

In 1932 the Public Commissariat of the Forest Industry, with a representative in Georgia, was formed under the Soviet Union governmental regulations, and all industrial forests were transferred to it. The purpose of these forests was to supply the industry with wood. Timber consumption was high, but transportation difficult, so logging was concentrated to areas which were easy to reach. A large share of the healthy productive trees were cut for industrial use, cutting rules were not observed and unsuitable selective cutting was practiced, as a result, the forestry situation deteriorated considerably. In 1939 the Inguri pulp and paper plant started its operations. During the third 5 year plan period (1938-42) extensive timber cutting started in Suaneti, Racha, Lechkhumi, Adzhara (and many other areas with previously virgin forests). During World War II wood deliveries from the rest of the Soviet Union were stopped and the burden increased on the local forests. In 1943 the Soviet Union government adopted a policy to divide the state forestland into groups and categories. Almost all (97.4%) of Georgia's forests were classified as belonging to group I. In these, soil protection, watershed protection, climate control and aesthetic values were the main priorities and final harvest was not permitted. The remaining 2.6% were classified as group II, (so-called productive-protected forests). These were all lowland forests, where wood production was a focus but where for protection reasons, there were clear restrictions on what could be done. This decision could have contributed greatly to the improvement of the situation in the forests of Georgia, but special regulations from the Soviet Union government still allowed for harvesting in the group I forests. The harvest of final cuts was from 1.6-2.0 million m³ (sob) per year up to 1965 when the harvest in the class I forests was stopped upon insistent requests from the local government of Georgia. In 1967, new rules for logging were developed for Georgia to curtail the obvious damage to the forest conditions in the country. It was seen as necessary to reduce the planned harvest to 535,000 m³ (sob) and this was later lowered to as little as 200,000 m³ (sob). In 1966 poorly stocked forests made up 21.5% of the forest area.

While the cutting volumes from final harvests has been continuously decreased over a long period, the volume from intermediate cuts instead increased. The volume of sanitation cutting went from 169,000 m³ (sob) in 1971 to 460,000 m³ (sob) in 1985. During the last 25 years the timber harvest was decreased many times. Recent years were characterized by the activation of natural disaster processes in certain mountainous areas of the country, which also affected the state of the country's forests. Recent intensive timber harvesting activities were unprecedented in the history of the country. This is mainly due to the almost complete reduction of the timber imports from Russia (which occurred after Georgia's independence). Imports of timber into Georgia from other regions used to be 2-2.5 million m³ (more than 85% of the country's requirements). To further exacerbate this situation, a sharp reduction of the imports of fuel was compensated by illegal harvesting of fuel wood by the population.

Graph 3
Dynamics and the forecast of wood utilization in Georgia
(1,000 m³)

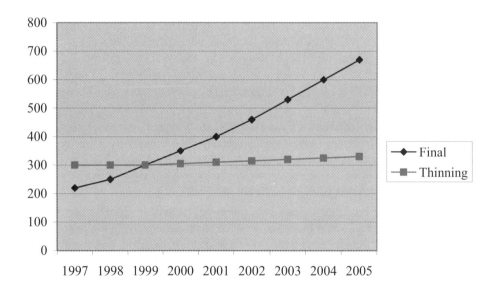

Forestry Legislation

After 70 years as part of the Soviet Union, Georgia has had a long transition period into a democratic and market oriented system. This transition process will not be finished for many years. Since the declaration of independence in April 1991, Georgia has dealt with numerous disasters and crises, like civil war, earthquakes, economic and energy crises (not to speak of the political instability and the pain to be transformed into a democratic market economy). Many laws and regulations have to be changed and created as a new structure of the government is put in place. Of course the forestry sector has not been a major priority as its economic contribution to the society has been rather small. In 1995 and 1997 some changes were made into existing Soviet Forest Code to regulate the activities and utilization of the Sate forest fund, as well as defining different forest categories and their utilization. The transition to a market economy revealed many weaknesses in the forestry branch which made it necessary to carry out urgent reforms to start economically, ecologically and socially acceptable forest management. For this reason Georgia had to come up with a new forest policy that would guarantee the protection of the forests' ecological, protective, and social functions, while at the same time providing the country with responsibly produced wood to improve the economy.

The most recent reform in Georgian forest legislation took place in 1999 by adoption of a new forest code. The new forest code lays a foundation for both institutional and policy reforms in the sector, and provides the legal basis for the organization, management and financing of Georgia's forestry. It sets the framework for a reorientation of the forestry sector from central planning to more market orientation. As one of the most important changes, the new code introduces the possibility to dedicate long-term user rights to the public or private bodies while land is still the property of the state. According to the code, Georgia's State Department of Forestry will not directly undertake commercial harvesting as it seeks to separate control and management functions, delegating the latter to private enterprises. It defines additional categories of protected forests, including those with special soil and watershed regulations, sensitive areas such as floodplains, steep slopes, sub-alpine forests, and those forest areas containing Red List endangered species. As part of the new forest code, which permits commercial logging on slopes of 35 degrees, the responsibilities for the issuance of logging licenses is also transferred from the Ministry of Environment to the SFD. The new forest code's major innovations include:

- Defining the principles of protection, sustainable development and management of the forests on the basis of the 1992 declaration (proclaiming focus on multiple use of forests and its environmental, economic, social and cultural dimensions) from the United Nations conference on environment and development in Rio de Janeiro. .
- Allowing for multiple forms of forest ownership (state, community, church and private).
- Allowing for long-term lease of forests and privatisation of forest management activities.
- Delineation and improvement of regulatory and oversight responsibilities between the State Forestry Department and the Ministry of Environment (though further work is needed to make the code operational and transparent).

At present almost all forest land is still owned by the State and though the approved forest code allows multiple forms of forest ownership, before carrying out this process, the law on privatisation should be drafted and adopted by the Government (after consideration of many other details including the experience of other countries). Georgia with a total area of 6.95 million ha of which 2.99 million ha are forest lands, and 2.77 million ha are forest covered (40% of the area of the country).

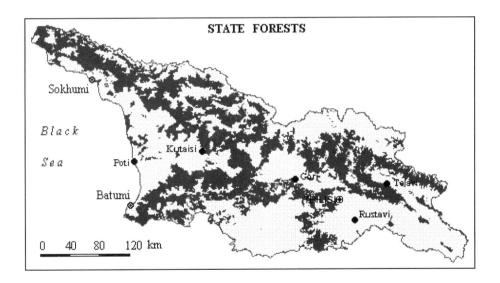

Graph 4
General Data of Georgian Forest Fund

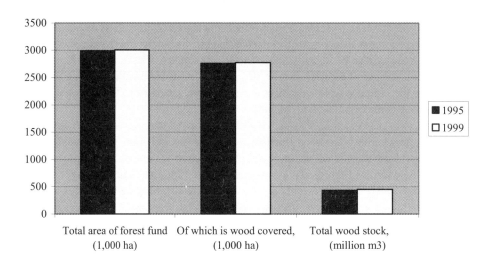

Total area of forest fund Of which is wood covered, Total wood stock,
(1,000 ha)   (1,000 ha)   (million m3)

Forest Resources

The total standing volume of wood is some 451 million m^3 (sob). With a population of 5.5 million, that gives a standing volume of just under 80 m^3 (sob) per person.

More than 2.5 million ha of the forests lands of Georgia are state property under the Forestry Department (according to 1999 statistics), smaller parts belong to the Department of Protected Areas, Reserves and Hunting (183,300 ha) and to the Mountain Forestry Research Institute (54,700 ha). For the majority of the nations forests, the Forestry Department is responsible for setting forest policy with the following priority issues: forest protection, reforestation and rational use of the forest resources.

Graph 5
Forest Distribution by administration category
(1,000 ha)

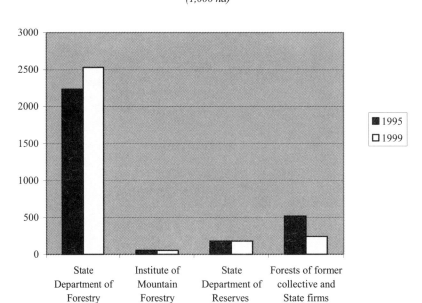

State   Institute of   State   Forests of former
Department of   Mountain   Department of   collective and
Forestry   Forestry   Reserves   State firms

The former kolkhoz owned forests are especially vulnerable to cutting activities. Their structure is easily destroyed, modification of species is speeded up, erosion processes are accelerated, and the forest forming plant species are substituted by satellite plant species and shrubs, or worse, the slopes are simply washed away.

Most of the Georgian forests according to the present classification are classed as mountain forests, and the majority of all timber will have to come from these forests. Mountain forests make up 98% of the forest area and have soil and water protection, conservation and recreation as main purposes. Harvesting is permitted in these forests, in the form of intermediate cuts and through various forms of selection harvests. The volume of the annual cut cannot exceed the annual growth increment. The main species for commercial use are beech, spruce and fir. Low elevation forest makes up less than 2% of the area and exists in both West and East Georgia. In the Alder dominated forests of the lowlands along the Black Sea ecological conditions permit clear cutting, but in other areas only selection systems can be used.

Graph 6
Forest Distribution According to protective Categories
(1,000 ha)

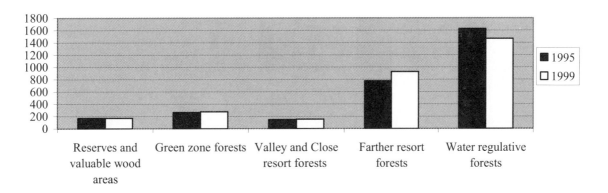

Only 7.3% of the forests are below 500m in elevation, 19.5% within 501-1000m, 35.5% within 1001-1500m, 30.7% within 1501-2000 m and 7.0% above 2000m. Above 1500 m. valuable trees like chestnut, beech and oak do not exist or have a very low growth.

Graph 7
Forest Distribution According to Altitude
(% of total)

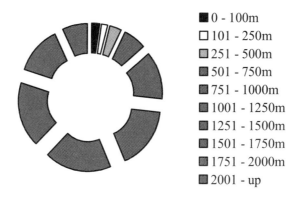

- 0 - 100m
- 101 - 250m
- 251 - 500m
- 501 - 750m
- 751 - 1000m
- 1001 - 1250m
- 1251 - 1500m
- 1501 - 1750m
- 1751 - 2000m
- 2001 - up

The forests of Georgia are distributed on the slopes of major and minor Caucasus and their distribution according to steepness of the slope is as follows: only 5.5% of the forests grows in areas up to 10 degrees, 16.5 % between 11-20, 16.6% between 21-25, 18.2% between 26-30, 19.6% between 31-35 and 23.6% on slopes above 36 degrees. On areas with slopes above 20 degrees, timber harvesting is difficult and costly, and at the same time the need for environmental protection increases.

Graph 8
Forest Distribution According to the Slope Percentage
(% of total)

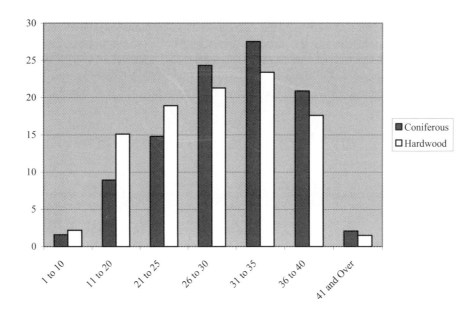

Factors like species, size, quality, and stocking levels (volume per ha) are important for determining a forest's economic potentials. The general information about Georgian forests is following: average tree height 22 m, mean diameter at breast height 36 cm, average stand density 0.54.

Graph 9
Forest Distribution According to the Density
(%)

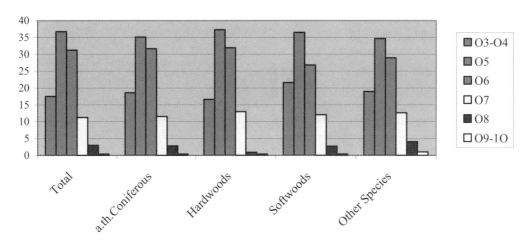

The mean standing volume is 176 m³ (sob/ha), mean standing volume in mature and over mature stands 244 m³ (sob/ha) and for coniferous only it is 288 m³ (sob/ha). Average stand age: overall 98 years, in coniferous stands 124 years. There is a lack of stands in the development classes of young and maturing stands. This is the result of poor forestry practices in the past. Mature and over mature forests exist mainly in hard to reach areas of West Georgia.

Graph 10
Forest Distribution According to the Bonitet (Site Productivity Class)
(%)

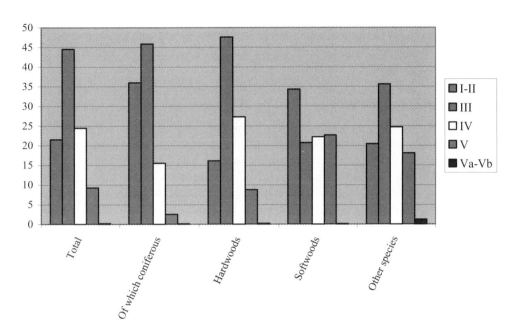

The forests are predominantly of broadleaved species. Of the forested area, beech covers 48.5 %, oaks 10.2%, fir 8.4%, hornbeam 6.6%, spruce 5.8%, pines 4.7%, alder 3,2%, chestnut 2.5% and mix of other tree and bush species the remaining 10.1%. During the glacial period plants of different species have been established in Georgia such as *Quercus pontica, Corylus iberica, Betula mingrelica, Staphylea colchica, Vaccinium arctostaphylos, Buxus colchica, Rhododendron ponticum, Hedera colchica*, etc. Together with 395 species of woody plants there are 183 forms and 91 variations. 151 plants (among them 61 woody plants) are included in the Red Book of Georgia.

In addition to wood and environmental functions, Georgian forests produce a great variety of non-wood products such as fruit, berries, nuts, bark, etc. These products come from more than 150 species, among them chestnut, cornelian cherry, pomegranate, Dog rose, various nuts like hazelnut and walnut, figs, blackberries, etc. These are important to people and wildlife. There are also some 100 species of edible mushrooms, of which only some 12-15 are regularly used. More than 60 native trees and bushes used for veterinary purposes, and the vegetative parts of more than 110 woody species are used in medicine. There is a great number of indigenous medicinal plants (more than 110 woody species) used for treating people and animals. Georgian forests are also rich in honey, and decorative plants. Out of 6350 species of known ferns, there are more than 4 100 species in Georgia.

Utilization of non-wood products by the people is free of charge. Utilization of some medicinal herbs and species that are included in the red book of Georgia is intensively used but in general the non-wood products are not used so much due to lack of financing and difficulties in collection and processing. There are no enterprises for processing mushrooms and berries.

There are 48 health resorts and some 200 other resort zones, two thirds of which are surrounded by forests set aside for the benefit of tourism and recreation. Within the Georgian forest estate are about 1700 ha of agricultural land, 6600 ha of meadows, 55600 ha grazing land, which if correctly used could bring considerable income. The potential for hunting in the forests are considerable. Hunting could be a source of income, both from national hunters and from foreign hunters (with proper promotion) if wildlife populations can be restored through management and the elimination of poaching.

There are up to 1000 plants, which are considered as endemic. Out of Georgia's 395 species of trees and 61 bushes, 61 naturally occur only in Georgia and another 43 only in the Caucasus region. The fauna of Georgia is also very rich. It includes some 330 birds, 100 mammals, and 59 amphibians and reptilians. Georgian Red Book includes 65 species of animals, 21 mammals, 34 birds and 10 amphibians and reptilians.

There are not many countries where the natural landscapes are so in harmony with history and culture as in Georgia. In Georgia's native forests there are fast growing giant species like the local fir (*Abies Nordmanniana*) of which there are stands holding 1500-2000 m³ sob/ha with trees up to 65 to 70 meter in height and 2 to 2.5 meter in diameter, and the beech (*Fagus Orientalis)*, which can grow 40-50 meter tall with a crown spread of 15-20 m, there are species of highly valuable wood like chestnut (*Castanea*), oak (*Quercus*), Zelkva (*Zelkova*), Box tree (*Buxus*), etc. The total area of virgin forests are 0.5 million ha.

Wood Utilization and Forest Industry

As stated earlier, in 1930-1950 there was intensive industrial timber cutting, which resulted in degradation in more than half of the forested area. About 500,000 ha of forests were lost, which resulted in the acceleration of erosion processes. After 1950, Georgia made efforts to reduce final felling from 1.5 million m³ to 453,000 m³, but since independence, the loss of wood imports has led timber processors to harvest Georgian forests. Illegally harvested timber, in the form of high-quality beech logs crossing the Turkish border accounts for about 6% of the total estimated harvest volume with nearly 60% of the annual forest harvest (or about 720,000 m³) in unrecorded fuel wood.

Illegal fuel wood harvests represent a serious threat to forest sustainability in some areas. This ongoing problem results from a desperate shortage of alternative energy sources and the lack of an effective control system. Primary fuel wood users are small households in the countryside. Fuel wood is harvested close to villages, which results in local degradation of adjacent forests. This problem is particularly severe in former kolkhoz and coppice forests, which, deprived of responsible management and protection, are gradually degraded. Better utilization of current harvests and effective enforcement show some promise in alleviating the problem, but it is unlikely to eliminate it. Forest operations can generate more fuel wood by utilizing logging residues such as branches, tops, stumps, and small trees (from tending cuts), dead trees, and wood from tree species of lesser industrial value. For example, branches and tops can constitute up to 30% of the total harvest volume and be used as fuel wood or wood chips. A recent study completed for TACIS indicated that the harvestable volume from sustainable forest management could be as high as 2 million m³ annually. Such harvests have the potential to meet the fuel wood demand and help to eliminate illegal and unsustainable fuel wood cuts. Before implementing this approach, it must be determined that it is economically rational and environmentally sound. On the economic side, high extraction costs will most likely eliminate stumps as a fuel wood source. On the environmental side, it must be considered that while logging always removes nutrients from the forest, small branches and twigs contain more nutrients than stem wood and their removal implies higher nutrient drainage rates. This in turn may have impacts on soils and site productivity. Removing wood residues may also change growing conditions for regenerated tree species and other flora and fauna species.

Prior to 1991, the Georgian paper and wood industries depended mainly on raw materials from other regions, primarily Russia. More than 95% of all raw materials came from abroad. Since 1991 all centralized wood import has been stopped. As for consumption of timber, the main share (50%) was used by the Ministries of Construction and Communal Economy for building purposes, furniture production took 20%, packing materials 14% and the rest was used for various other purposes.

The forest sector made up 4-5% of the GDP during the period of central planning. Before 1990 within the sector, logging counted for 14%, the wood processing industry for 69% and the pulp and paper industry for 17%. Of the wood processing industry in 1980 and 1990, sawmills made up 10.4% and 9.0%, furniture production 55% and 60%, building details 12.1 % and 11.0%, packaging material 7.2% and 6.0% and other wood processing 15.3% and 14.0%.

Prior to 1991, most of the wood processing industry was under the Ministry of Timber and Wood Working Industry, Its share of the total production volume was 70.9% and it controlled 37.3% of the enterprises. Wood working industries also existed within 11 other Ministries.

The extraction of wood during the period 1970-1980 dropped by 40% from the level of 1961. The extraction dropped further during the 1980s to a level of about 30% of what was extracted during the 1960s. From 1970 on, the intermediate cutting increased, and from 1980 it made up the major part of the total extraction. Since 1990, the general cuttings have been reduced to only 200,000 m^3 (until 1970 that type of cutting was more than 1,000,000 m^3 per year). In 1967 new rules for logging were developed for Georgia to address the obvious damage to the forest condition in the country. In 1966 poorly stocked forests made up 21.5% of the entire forest area. As a result, the planned harvest of industrial wood was reduced to 535 000 m^3 (sob), and this was later reduced to 200,000 m^3 (sob). This also decreased the fuel wood production from general cutting, but the extraction from sanitary cuttings increased manifold

The wood working industry suffered from the fact that there was no supporting industry in Georgia producing products like synthetic glues, paints and varnishes, technical glass, plastic, material for stuffing of soft furniture, etc. The wood working industry had no basis for success during the transition period and is still not ready to work under economic independence. The production facilities have to buy materials on the open market, in small quantities and at prices significantly higher than wholesale prices. The timber supplies from mainly the eastern parts of Russia were of course not economically efficient, prices were artificially low and what was paid for transport did not cover the actual cost.

During the period of 1994-1996, the forest industry was almost completely privatised, with complete privatisation of the timber processing, furniture producing and paper industry belonging to the Industry department (the former ministry of Timber and Wood Working Industry and the Georgian Paper Industry Organization) fully privatised by January 1, 1997. Twenty-four enterprises have been made into joint stock companies, 4 changed into limited partnership owned companies (companies with a few individual owners) and only 3 remained in the state management structure. Of the enterprises that were under the Ministry of Construction and other organizations, 70% have been privatised. The privatisation process was carried out during a time of economic crisis and it was a painful process. While the formal process of privatisation was carried out, a large share of the stock went unsold. Neither commercial organizations nor private individuals showed much interest in buying what was offered, in spite of vouchers which gave 30% rebates on the price of shares for private individuals. For most of the companies only 23-45% of the shares have been sold, and just eight small to medium-sized companies have been completely sold. The unsold stock is held by the Ministry of State Property Management and is still on the market.

In Georgia there was one integrated pulp and paper mill and one paper mill. The pulp production stopped in 1990. Today there is only a small production of paperboard, based on waste paper. It is assumed that in the short to medium term neither the Inguri Pulp & Paper Industrial Complex (which has undergone restructuring and has been transformed into 15 independent joint stock companies) nor the Tbilisi Paper Mill will restart any production of pulp and paper. Today a discussion is going on about merging some of the units into a new organization. No expansion of the pulping industry is foreseen in Georgia for the next 10-year period, and no demand for wood fuel is therefore included in the wood fuel balance. At present, no fuel chips are produced or used in Georgia.

The demand for locally produced furniture also failed for the same reasons. Imported furniture is becoming more common and popular because of a better design and often-lower prices. A further reason is that during the last 7 years the furniture industry has had no money to modernize its equipment. Much of the old equipment is no longer functioning since it has not been used for several years. The demand for furniture from 1991 to 1996 was reduced by 85 to 90%.

The fibreboard and particleboard industries have comparably high-energy consumption both in the form of electric power as well as heat. Some quantities of wood waste that can be used as fuel are produced in these industries, but additional fuel has to be supplied from other sources, e.g. sawmill wood waste, logging residues, or stem wood from trees of non-industrial value. No reliable statistics on specific energy consumption of the board factories in Georgia are available. Currently, bark, chips, sawdust and other wood residues are only marginally used for energy purposes. The majority of the energy consumed within a sawmill is for the drying of the sawn wood. No accurate and reliable figures for the average specific heat consumption per m^3 of sawn wood produced are currently available for Georgia.

The total annual extraction of fuel wood from 1991 onward is difficult to calculate as there is a large amount of private, unofficial cutting of household fuel wood which is not accounted for (officially only some 250 000 m^3 of fuel wood is produced annually).

Graph 11
Georgia forest industry production 1940-1995
(1,000 m³)

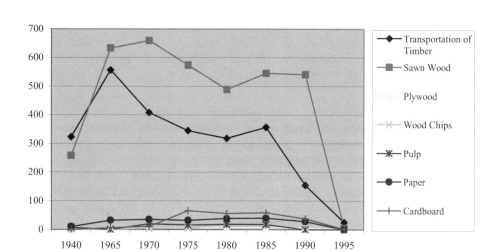

At present, the biggest of the old enterprises are the most inefficient and unprofitable. They must be reorganized, re-capitalized, and in some cases possibly liquidated. As mentioned above, after the breakdown of the Soviet centralized planning and distribution system and during the transition, the forest industry lost its customer base. House construction stopped, and the traditional big consumers (especially for furniture), like the public construction sector, the educational system, the cultural and medical sectors, resorts and hotels, all became insolvent. The distribution system and transportation system also had problems with poor maintenance, lack of energy and a shortage of trucks. In fact transport costs became so high that it was not profitable to transport timber and deliver finished products. The solution for the revival of the Georgian forest industry is finding stable and strong markets for their products.

Prices

International experience shows that a competitive forestry sector requires a system for pricing of standing timber, which makes the wood producers able to cover all costs for wood production. Many countries rich in forests, have artificially reduced the production costs with subsidies (to wood producers or for energy or transport) or by protecting the market with trade barriers. This has often resulted in mismanagement of the wood working industry, non-economic distribution of resources, excessive industrial capacity, and/or a low level of investments.

In Georgia the net wood value (both industrial and fuel wood) is formulated from Stumpage tax (price), expenditure for harvesting and processing, and market price. The basis for stumpage taxation is provided in tax code (art.194,2, see Annex G). The stumpage tax is calculated using official market prices identified by the Ministry of Economy, Trade and Industry with recommendations by the State Forestry Department according to art. 27,10 of the tax code. The current official market prices are provided in *annex* G for different wood groups, different wood quality and standing trees location (distance from main road/railroad). Table 1 provides different coefficients (in percentage) for calculating stumpage tax. The stumpage tax for the best quality Beech trees with a diameter of more then 25 cm, and with the closest location to main roads (stumpage, category 1) is 33.8 GEL per m³ (about $15.36). This is the highest stumpage tax for the most utilized wood specie in Georgia. The Stumpage tax for fuel wood of the same stands is 6.5 GEL ($3) per m³.

The harvesting and transport costs for industrial and fuel wood are calculated according to the production standards and current cost levels in Georgia. The harvesting and transport costs for fuel wood are calculated between 26.88 GEL/ m^3 and 22.57 GEL/ m^3 depending on species and means of terrain transport. Harvesting and transportation costs for conifers are about 1 GEL lower per m^3, and the animal transportation costs are about 3 GEL less per m^3. The terrain transport distance is assumed to be 3 km, and truck transport distance 35 km. Logging costs for the production and export of high quality beech logs are provided in a*nnex G.*

The end user normally does the fuel wood preparation, and no costs are shown. If the crosscutting and splitting is done manually by hired personnel, the production can be estimated at about two man-hours per m^{3}s or about 2 GEL per m^3. The market price for fuel wood varies depending on location. In Tbilisi the market price can be as high as 25-40GEL / m^3 ($10-$18) while in the countryside the cost can be as low as 5 GEL/ m^{3}s ($2.2) at roadside.

Beech saw timber stumpage value is derived from beech saw timber export prices, which represent the maximum price level currently attainable in Georgia. The stumpage value per m^3 is calculated by subtracting corresponding cost components. At the Georgian border, beech saw timber is priced at on average$120/m^3. Stumpage tax, logging costs, truck or rail shipping costs, and miscellaneous costs equals on average about $83/m^3. Subtracting these costs from the border price yields a beech saw timber stumpage value of approximately $37/m^3 (before accounting for a business profit and a risk premium). Saw timber of other species is considerably lower in value and its stumpage value is estimated at roughly $25/m^3. For comparison to the finished products, the prices for wood products, (particularly export prices of the best quality Beech particle board), are between $250 to $450 per m^3.

Trade and Timber Markets

Most countries conduct wood trade in various ways (auctions, competitive trade, volumetric sale, sales on the basis of estimating the value) with the purpose of transferring the appropriate share of the proceeds from the purchaser to the owner. Georgia has almost no practical experience in selling wood in international or even national markets according to these market rules. Competitive trade under fair conditions can maximize the income of the forest owner, but it is not always the best method, because other economic, social and environmental values are not taken into consideration.

Since Georgian independence, timber has received serious attention as a way to get exports started. The biggest potential is for beech wood, but demand is also good for fir and pine. Wood market information indicates that wood from traditional suppliers may be going down (partly for environmental reasons) and this could help Georgia get a place in the international wood market. Wood exports could become an important source of income for the country. During the early transition years, roundwood exports were not controlled, and for this reason, temporary measures were introduced (at the urgent requests of the general population), such as a temporary ban on final felling (1998-1999) and numerous temporary bans on log export. These restrictions were aimed at reducing illegal felling, and to protect the local timber processing industry.

Timber trade statistics in Georgia are incomplete and often provide contradicting information, as a result, foreign trade sources need to be used to assess timber exports from Georgia. Timber trade statistics in Georgia indicate that in 1999 Georgia (excluding Abkhazia) exported from 71,000 to 88,000 m^3 to Turkey These exports were dominated by beech, which accounted for 92% of their volume. The total wood exports to all countries from Georgia (excluding Abkhazia) were estimated from 114,000 to 142,000 m^3. To supply such an amount of high quality timber, it was necessary to harvest 240,000 to 300,000 thousand m^3. While this amount does not exceed the official allowable harvest figures, it considerably exceeds the volume of allowable harvested saw timber. According to statistics from the Customs Department, Georgia exported about 55,000 m^3 in 1999. Since 1997 exports declined by nearly 20,000 m^3. These statistics also indicate that logs, which on average constitute nearly 70% of trade volume, dominate the exports (more comprehensive information regarding 1999 exports are available from the Statistics Department). Official trade statistics provided by the Statistical Department of Turkey indicate that Turkey imported from Georgia about 112 thousand m^3 of wood in 1999. Beech dominated timber imports, accounting for about 92% of the volume.

A comparison of these numbers with the customs statistics from Georgia indicates that for 1999 the Georgian statistics:

1. underestimate timber exports by up to nearly 60% for the upper bound import values in Turkey.
2. do not provide or underestimate timber export values.
3. indicate opposite trade dynamics.
4. provide similar timber import/export structure information (log to processed wood ratio roughly equal 30/70).

Beyond that, it is very difficult to make further conclusions. At this time, the Statistics Department data are not used in the analysis unless the identified errors are corrected. Other imported species include pine, spruce, and hornbeam. Sawlogs accounted for about 65% of imported volume, and roughly processed timber (squared logs, planks, etc.) for 35%. The total value of timber imports equalled about $13.5 million. Average prices were $117/m^3 for logs and $128/m^3 for semi-processed timber. Nearly the same prices for logs and semi-processed timber indicate only rough processing and/or timber quality issues. In case more advanced processing took place and timber was of high quality, the average price of processed dried wood is much higher, (potentially reaching the range of $600-$900/m^3 for beech).

A monthly breakdown of timber imports indicate the seasonality of the timber trade with the smallest amount of timber imported in January and February. These months are generally known for poor weather conditions, which make logging in Georgia expensive and difficult because of the lack of appropriate logging equipment and poor road conditions. Timber imports peak during the summer months (June, July and August).

Institutions

There are several state agencies responsible for forest policy and strategy as well as management of the state forests. These are Ministry of Environment, State Forestry Department, State Department of Protected Areas, Ministry of Agriculture and Food, etc.

The Ministry of Environment (*68a, Kostava str. Tbilisi. tel. 995 32 230 664, fax. 995 32 943 670, Minister Ms. Nino Chkhobadze)*, established in 1991 is the main agency responsible for environmental protection and the regulation of natural resource use. It has approximately 2,000 employees. The Department of Biodiversity Protection is responsible for biodiversity conservation within MoE, including formulation and implementation of biodiversity policy, integrating biodiversity into sectoral policies and programs, and in guiding and coordinating the activities of the regional offices. The Ministry of Environment also provides the following services:

*   Reviews sectoral plans.
*   Approves forest management plans.
*   Monitors forest operations to ensure they conform with permit conditions(in accordance with environment laws in force).
*   Establishes quota on nature resources use.
*   Confirms the license rights and issues them.
*   Provides in sphere of nature resources use the creation of Database of information Bank and functioning of information system.
*   Works out the organization of State Cadastre.
*   Prepares "Red Data Book" and "Red list".
*   Works out the organization of environmental monitoring system.
*   Provides State control on the environment.

State Forestry Department (SFD) (*9 Mindeli str. Tbilisi. tel. 995 32 304 377. fax. 995 32 320 549, Chairman – Mr. Givi Japaridze)* is responsible for developing forest strategy and policy, as well as oversight of the management of the forest estate. Its Chairman reports directly to the President of Georgia and holds a ministerial rank. The SFD is composed of a central office in Tbilisi, 54 district offices, three parks and three nurseries. The total staff is 2,637 people, of whom 63 are located at the headquarters in Tbilisi. In addition, there are nine "forest enterprises" with full managerial autonomy, but dependant on the SFD for their financing. The most important among them is *Lesoproject*, which undertakes forest inventory and management plans. The total (received) budget of the SFD, including the forest enterprises, was Lari 2.8 million (US$ 2.2 million) for 1998 – of which three-quarters was directly provided by the Ministry of Finance. The other source of income consisted of revenue from sales by the district offices of wood and non-wood products (e.g. logs, fuel wood, fruits and berries). Close to 70% of the SFD's annual expenditures in 1998 (Lari 4.8 million) was utilized for staff salaries.

Current SFD functions and responsibilities are as follow:
- To improve the ecological and economic efficiency of forest production.
- To support scientific research.
- To make proposals concerning the implementation of an anti-monopoly and privatisation policies in the forestry sector.
- To carry out an inventory of the state forest resource base.
- In collaboration with the Ministry of Environmental Protection and National Resources, to regulate resource utilization.
- To initiate and draft projects of legislative and normative acts.

A Brief Description of Forest Enterprises Involved with the Forest Department

Forest Inspection. This organization has a mandate to monitor forestry activities and evaluate environmental impacts according to existing rules and regulations. Funds are provided from the national budget. It has a staff of 12 professionals.

Wood Construction. This is an enterprise working under contract for the SFD. It carries out mainly civil works related to road construction. It has a staff of 12 professionals.

Administrative and Supplementary Building. This enterprise supplies office materials, furniture and small equipment to the SFD under contract.

Forest Seed Selection. Working under contract for the SFD, this group collects, treats (cleans, dries, packs), and sells seeds. It employs 31 people including 7 professionals and 3 technicians. Its main source of income is the national budget through the SFD.

Forest Seed Testing Station. This enterprise of 8 persons, mainly professionals, conducts germination tests to check seed quality. All income comes from the national budget through contracts with the SFD.

Trade Company "Metkeve". As the name suggests, this is a trading company working under contract for the SFD. It supports the SFD through its commercial activities.

Forest Management Project. Its mandate consists of "cadastre" (surveying) activities (road lay out, block lay out, etc.). It has a staff of 42 persons, including 33 professionals.

Lesoproject. This is a State-owned enterprise. Its mandate consists of carrying out forest inventories and preparing forest management plans. It has a staff of 152 persons of whom 93 are professionals and 26 technicians. The majority of its income is derived from contracts with the SFD.

State Department for the Protected Areas. This organisation has the same levels as the Forestry Department. It is a small organization with a total staff of 17 in Tbilisi and 450 others assigned to individual protected areas. The Department is charged with oversight of the existing protected areas (currently 1 national park, 13 strict nature reserves and 5 managed nature reserves). With the adoption of the new categories of protected areas, the DPA has additional functions, including the development of legislation and policy related to revenue generation, such as park charges, development of eco-tourism, and management of recreational use.

Functions of **Ministry of Agriculture and Food** (*41, Kostava str. Tbilisi, tel. 995 32 990 272, fax. 995 32 933 300)* are land protection and rational use, soil reconstruction, domestic animal and plant genetic resources protection, renewal and control on seeds and seedlings quality.

There are two research institutes as well, dealing with natural resources; the ***Mountain Forestry Research Institute (MFRI)*** and the ***Institute of Plant Protection***, both under the jurisdiction of the Georgian Academy of Sciences. The Forestry Research Institute is directly involved in forestry research whereas the Institute of Plant Protection mainly deals with agriculture but is also involved in pest control as it relates to forestry.

At present it is planned to re-organize the Government of Georgia. According to the proposed re-organization plan, the number of Ministries could be reduced by 10. It is assumed that the State Department of Forestry, Department of Protected Areas and the Department of Geology will be merged with the Ministry of Environment.

Outlook

Georgia has been shaken dramatically over the last decade. Ecological and social problems made it urgent to carry out reforms in the forest sector. State organizations have to gradually stop carrying out commercial activities and instead allow market forces to efficiently re-distribute the resources. The present forest industries cannot and should not be utilized in their present forms, as machinery and production methods are outdated and forestry staff needs further training. The present shortage of funds for retooling, maintenance and repair, a challenged transportation infrastructure, labour issues, as well as the energy shortage, have contributed to an extremely low utilization of installed capacity.

The current situation of Georgian forests is characterized by a virtual stoppage of appropriate forest management, uncontrolled and increasingly unsustainable harvesting of timber resources in a number of areas, and uncontrolled hunting and grazing in forestlands across the country. The result of this is an undermining of watershed protection, wildlife habitat, and the functionality and biodiversity of the Georgian forest.

To improve the situation and realize higher forest values, the government should work on creating conditions in which resources are allocated to efficient and environmentally sustainable uses. Among other things, this would include total re-organization of the whole forestry system and its institutions, appropriate land allocation for protective and production uses, and on production areas, match investments with returns to maximize timber values. Government should ensure that forest users recognize the value of the forest through appropriate prices, regulations, and rewards. The government must also assure appropriate funding for forest management and protection. Better enforcement funding would help to limit illegal forest uses, and rewards would help to increase sustainable forest uses.

At the present time, roles, responsibilities, and authorities between the Ministry of Environment, State Department of Forestry and the Department of Protected Areas, as well as the other related forest sector institutions are confusing, duplicative and even contradictory. This is partly a result of the shift from the rigid Soviet institutional style toward a more integrated approach to environmental management, which reflects different institutional models for environmental policy and regulation, as well as the opportunities presented by increased donor resources available for environmental projects. Due to the new forest code, management of forests is delegated primarily to the private sector, leaving SDF with a regulatory mandate. The infusion of donor resources supporting biodiversity conservation and forestry also offers significant opportunities to clarify roles, relationships, and build partnerships among government institutions. The lack of appropriate forest maintenance operations and illegal harvesting are the most pressing issues that threaten to diminish the size and quality of the Georgian forests if allowed to go on unchecked. Illegal harvesting – a result of high international demand for the quality timber that is so abundant in Georgia and weak enforcement – is carried out in such a way that it is damaging the environment, notably the watercourses, soils, wildlife and ground vegetation. At present 60% of the annual forest harvest is estimated as unrecorded fuel wood. The main harvesting is around population centres and is clearly visible, especially outside Tbilisi, where its adjacent hills have been stripped bare within the last five years. This has lead to water run off issues such as, ruts, soil erosion and soil degradation. The fuel wood harvest continues to this day. At this stage, this situation is difficult to stop or monitor, as the ordinary citizens have fallen on hard times and need fuel for cooking, heating water, bathing and keeping warm. This problem is particularly severe in former kolkhoz and coppice forests, which, deprived of responsible management and protection, are gradually being severely degraded.

The most immediate threat to Georgian forests is the harvesting of fuel wood. Declining GDP, rising poverty and the decline in energy subsidies for fossil fuels (which has led to greatly increased use of fuel wood). The primary responses to the illegal fuel wood harvests include (1) alternative fuels, (2) energy saving measures, (3) better utilization of the current timber harvest combined with better enforcement of forest laws, and (4) increased timber harvests. The first two choices do not directly relate to forestry, and will not discussed any further, other than to note that in the current economic situation the extensive use of alternative energy sources is unlikely. Better utilization of current harvests and effective enforcement of current laws show some promise in alleviating the problem, but given its scale, it is unlikely to eliminate it. The primary sources of additional fuel wood from the current harvests are forestry operations and wood residues from the forest industry. Forest operations can generate more fuel wood by utilizing logging residues such as branches, tops, stumps, dead trees, and wood from tree species of lesser industrial value (including small trees from thinning cuts). Before implementing these approaches however, it must be determined that it is economically rational and environmentally sound. Finally, the last option would be to increase harvest levels. This could help to alleviate the problem provided that increased harvests are sustainable. This may be achievable by eliminating unsustainable fuel wood cutting near villages, and cutting more in areas where forest conditions support sustainable fuel wood harvests.

Increasing the harvest level to 1million m³ would substantially contribute to the generation of higher revenues as well. But only after considering the costs of these increased harvests would it be possible to determine if and by how much net benefits would increase. While timber revenues would increase, timber harvests could likely cause soil erosion and degradation of water conditions and lower tourism/recreational values. It should be recognized that on some environmentally sensitive sites such as steep slopes, ravines, and gorges, timber harvests would be unprofitable under any conditions. On other sites essential for biodiversity, wildlife habitat, soil and watershed protection, environmental costs may well exceed timber harvest benefits. Therefore, it must be determined how forestland should be allocated to environmental and productive uses and how much timber should be produced, applying economic, environmental, and social criteria.

Timber harvest decisions are one of many that guide timber management. Harvested forests need to be regenerated and managed, affectively by keeping in mind the benefits and costs associated with the entire forest rotation. Therefore, it is also necessary to examine the criteria guiding silvicultural operations, harvest rotation length, and harvest level determination (especially in relation to market conditions). Potentially, on less productive lands total timber management costs could exceed timber benefits, and it may be reasonable to remove this forestland from timber production and allocate it to the provision of environmental services.

Timber harvests may also generate some positive non-timber benefits. Logging provides better access to forests helping to increase hunting or foodstuff collection. Timber harvest may also generate some social benefits. This is because logging operations will likely create some employment opportunities and create some infrastructures (roads, bridges, etc.) which can be used by and benefit local communities. Finally, timber harvests provide some forest protection benefits by removing damaged or diseases trees which will increase the forest's resistance against diseases and damages (such as fire) by improving the forest structure.

It must be noted though, that even when timber harvesting can be accomplished with good silvicultural results and without any environmental damages, it would not necessarily imply that timber should be harvested. The decision to harvest will depend on timber prices, distance to markets, road construction, equipment, and fuel costs. The economic evaluation of timber harvest will change along with evolving market conditions. When prices are low, harvest may not be profitable. But this may change as prices increase, and a previously unprofitable harvest may yield positive net benefits and vice versa. Logging costs are also closely related to regulations guiding environmental protection. More stringent regulations usually require more advanced and therefore more expensive logging technologies.

After the existing wood processing industry is restructured, the development of efficient domestic processing may help increase timber values. High quality and thus high valued wood products demanded from the international market will permit the industry to afford higher than current timber prices. While there are some signals that joint venture operations are taking hold, there is a long way to go for a full recovery. In order to produce high quality beech products and receive high prices, wood-drying facilities (currently absent in Georgia), and modern processing technologies are required. Their acquisition requires substantial investment capital, which is not available in Georgia. In such a situation foreign investment is a viable alternative. Foreign investors can provide not only the required technologies, but also marketing expertise and access to global trade networks that will guarantee the highest prices for Georgian wood. Modern technologies also enable production of high quality engineered wood products from lower quality timber, which would again increase value. It is essential to attract foreign investment that can provide capital and know-how. Domestic industries need to ensure the highest quality processing and should remain competitive by the virtue of close resource location, cheap labour, and low taxes.

Even assuming a rapid flow of investment into domestic wood processing, some time has to pass before a modern processing industry is developed. The question is then; what can be done today to ensure efficient timber utilization that generates the highest possible values? A possible response to this concern is the development of more effective and freer trade policies. Timber in Georgia is much cheaper than in other countries and smuggling yields a substantial premium. Restrictive trade policies may force this outcome by separating domestic and international markets, and maintaining artificially low domestic prices. Free trade polices would help to bring domestic prices closer to international prices and therefore reduce or even eliminate incentives for smuggling. Such an approach appears much more effective when compared to calls for even more stringent controls that have failed so far.

Bringing domestic prices to international market prices would increase stumpage values. In this vein, a monitoring system for wood market price trends should be established, that would be officially published and stored in a forest information system.

Erosion is a major problem, especially in the agricultural sector, but also in the forest areas. Most of the forests are on rather steep slopes, which are easily eroded. Erosion can be aggravated by over exploitation of forests, neglect of regeneration forests and intensive grazing. Forests fulfil important watershed management and protection functions, notably soil protection and water retention that have economic implications. Excessive tree cutting and grazing in forest areas result in forest degradation, which expose the soil to the eroding effects of water and wind. It's widely believed that the current level of grazing in forest areas is damaging much of the forest, and is contributing to soil degradation, erosion, and threatens biodiversity. Soil erosion leads to reduced forest productivity and sedimentation of waterways and reservoirs, which in turn results in decreased effectiveness of irrigation and hydroelectric investments. The loss of forest also decreases water retention capacity, which in turn reduces agricultural productivity on adjacent lands and may lead to more frequent and larger floods, causing further damage and requiring increased flood control investments.

Road construction plays an important role in the analysis as it is directly related to timber harvest levels and values. The SFD claims that substantial road construction and maintenance investments are required to increase harvest up to the desired volume. These existing surface roads generally are of low standards, which not only limit their usefulness but also raise environmental concerns regarding soil erosion and water pollution. Better roads are needed that would allow operations during the whole year and that will be equipped with better soil erosion and water pollution control features. Their construction must be economically justified and environmentally responsible. Such roads will help to schedule harvests according to market demand and preserve timber quality by using better logging technologies, such as cable systems, and by removing harvested timber promptly from the forest. New roads may also increase the value of non-wood forest uses such as hunting and make some sanitary and conservation operations easier to conduct. Roads are currently constructed by loggers who secure a five-year cutting license limited to 25 ha and 100 m^3/ha annual harvest. This approach does not provide sufficient incentives for the construction and maintenance of higher standard roads because construction costs are very high compared to the value of harvest. There are basically three solutions to this problem. The first leaves road construction to private enterprises and provides incentives for higher standard road construction. This can be done by increasing the area and the period for which a license is awarded (thus increasing harvest values and creating better opportunities for recapturing road construction costs). This would also help to stimulate investment in modern logging technologies. The second solution would be to set lower license fees (thus increasing profit margins and investment funds). The state should develop and enforce appropriate road construction and maintenance standards .The third approach has the state taking a more active role in road construction and providing required funding. Creating better access to high quality timber will allow the state to charge higher license fees that would offset road construction costs. The government could obtain funding by increasing timber license fees.

Georgian forests are particularly rich in non-wood products. During the present difficult period, the population, who cannot afford to buy expensive medicine, often uses medicinal herbs and plants. There is certainly a great potential to develop some of the non-wood forest products. The production possibilities and the quality of the various products have to be assessed. Georgian society derives significant benefit by collecting forest food products, notably mushrooms, nuts, berries wild fruits, and medicinal plants for personal use and trade.

Georgians practice hunting and fishing activities widely for recreational and food purposes. It is believed that current wildlife harvest levels are unsustainable, and laws protecting endangered species against poachers are not well enforced. Furthermore, it is believed that currently hunting visits to Georgia by foreigners are rare. The Forest Department has made a proposal to develop hunting reserves as a way to sustainably manage hunting and attract foreign hunters to generate revenues from trophy fees, hunting guide fees, and payments made for goods and services by locals to hunter tourists. Georgians can derive significant recreational and tourism benefits from daily and multi-day recreational visits to forest areas. The establishment of national parks in forest areas would help conserve forests and channel revenues to government for management and conservation. Nature in Georgia is exceptionally rich and varied. In the inaccessible areas, high in the mountains there are still areas practically untouched by man. There is a need to improve the protection of these unique forest wild-lands which contain such a wide variety of animal and plant species. These resources constitute a valuable tourism development potential and will help local communities earn revenues from tourists, which is an alternative to unsustainable forest use such as overgrazing and poaching.

The previous isolation of Georgia from the West and the limited experience of market economic relations suggest that technical assistance to the forestry sector is crucial.

References

Georgia in Figures. A concise statistical handbook. 1970-2001. Tbilisi

The State Program of Forest Sector Revival in Georgia (1997-2005) SFD. Tbilisi

Georgian Forest Strategy – Part of Georgian Environment Protection Strategy Plan. WB. 1997

Georgia. National Forestry Development Program. WB/FAO. 1999

Technical Assistance at Industry and Consumer Level, Georgia. TACIS Project EGE/95/02. 1998

Georgia. Communal Forest Pilot Project. KFW. 2001

Some Data on Georgian Forests. SFD. Tbilisi. 2001

Georgian Economic Trends. TACIS. 2001

Total Economic Valuation of Georgian Forests. WB 2000

Annexes

Annex A. Demographic Situation in Georgia

Table 1
Population of Georgia, 1960-1997
(1,000 people)

Year	Population	of which		%		Males	Females	Females per 1,000 males
		Urban	Rural	Urban	Rural			
1960	4 129.2	1 744.4	2 384.8	42.2	57.8	1 908	2 221	1 164
1965	4 450.0	2 026.3	2 423.7	45.5	54.5	2 074	2 376	1 146
1970	4 686.4	2 239.8	2 446.6	47.8	52.2	2 202	2 484	1 128
1975	4 895.4	2 434.0	2 461.4	49.7	50.3	2 306	2 589	1 123
1980	5 052.8	2 634.8	2 418.0	52.1	47.9	2 375	2 678	1 128
1981	5 093.2	2 670.8	2 422.4	52.4	47.6	2 397	2 696	1 125
1982	5 132.5	2 711.1	2 421.4	52.8	47.2	2 417	2 716	1 124
1983	5 176.5	2 751.9	2 424.6	53.2	46.8	2 441	2 736	1 121
1984	5 220.0	2 791.3	2 428.7	53.5	46.5	2 463	2 757	1 119
1985	5 264.1	2 833.7	2 430.4	53.8	46.2	2 486	2 778	1 117
1986	5 309.8	2 876.8	2 433.0	54.2	45.8	2 511	2 799	1 115
1987	5 355.5	2 925.2	2 430.3	54.6	45.4	2 535	2 821	1 113
1988	5 396.7	2 975.1	2 421.6	55.1	44.9	2 557	2 840	1 111
1989	5 443.4	3 035.8	2 407.6	55.8	44.2	2 581	2 862	1 109
1990	5 456.1	3 058.2	2 397.9	56.1	43.9	2 590	2 866	1 107
1991	5 464.2	3 073.0	2 391.2	56.2	43.8	2 595	2 869	1 106
1992	5 462.8	3 068.1	2 394.7	56.2	43.8	2 581	2 839	1 100
1993	5 447.1	3 048.8	2 398.3	56.0	44.0	2 576	2 829	1 098
1994	5 433.5	3 030.2	2 403.3	55.8	44.2	2 571	2 820	1 097
1995	5 417.7	3 015.0	2 402.7	55.7	44.3	2 563	2 812	1 097
1996	5 416.0	3 012.2	2 403.8	55.6	44.4	2 563	2 810	1 096
1997	5 423.6	3 014.7	2 408.9	55.6	44.4	2 587	2 837	1 097

Source: The State Department of Statistics

Table 2
Population Movements, 1960-1997
(1000 people)

Year	1 January population	Live Births	Total Deaths	Natural increase per annum	Net Migration per annum	Total increase per annum	Natural increase	Net Migration	Total increase
1960	4 129 200	102 870	27 015	75.9	-15.2	60.7	1.8	-0.4	1.5
1965	4 450 000	94 987	31 291	63.7	-8.8	54.9	1.4	-0.2	1.2
1970	4 686 400	90 207	34 283	55.9	-11.4	44.5	1.2	-0.2	0.9
1975	4 895 400	89 712	39 292	50.4	-25.8	24.6	1.0	-0.5	0.5
1980	5 052 800	89 458	43 346	46.1	-5.7	40.4	0.9	-0.1	0.8
1981	5 093 200	92 501	43 961	48.5	-9.2	39.3	1.0	-0.2	0.8
1982	5 132 500	91 784	42 734	49.1	-5.1	44.0	1.0	-0.1	0.9
1983	5 176 500	92 660	43 301	49.4	-5.9	43.5	1.0	-0.1	0.8
1984	5 220 000	95 841	45 787	50.1	-6.0	44.1	1.0	-0.1	0.8
1985	5 264 100	97 739	46 153	51.6	-5.9	45.7	1.0	-0.1	0.9
1986	5 309 800	98 155	46 354	51.8	-6.1	45.7	1.0	-0.1	0.9
1987	5 355 500	94 595	46 332	48.3	-7.1	41.2	0.9	-0.1	0.8
1988	5 396 700	91 905	47 544	44.4	-0.2	44.2	0.8	0.0	0.8
1989	5 443 300	91 138	47 077	44.1	-28.9	15.2	0.8	-0.5	0.3
1990	5 456 100	92 815	45 946	46.9	-38.8	8.1	0.9	-0.7	0.1
1991	5 464 200	89 091	46 473	42.6	-44.0	-1.4	0.8	-0.8	0.0
1992	5 462 800	76 631	46 762	25.9	-41.6	-15.7	0.5	-0.8	-0.3
1993	5 447 100	61 594	48 938	12.7	-26.3	-13.6	0.2	-0.5	-0.2
1994	5 433 500	57 311	41 596	15.7	-31.5	-15.8	0.3	-0.6	-0.3
1995	5 417 700	56 341	37 874	18.5	-20.2	-1.7	0.3	-0.4	0.0
1996	5 416 000	53 669	34 414	19.3	-11.7	7.6	0.4	-0.2	0.1
1997	5 423 600	52 020	36 570	15.5	-0.5	15.0	0.3	0.0	0.3

Source: The State Department of Statistics

Annex B. Social – Economic Situation

Table 1

POVERTY and SOCIAL	Georgia	Europe & Central Asia	Low-income
1999			
Population, mid-year *(millions)*	5.5	475	2,417
GNP per capita *(Atlas method, US$)*	620	2,150	410
GNP *(Atlas method, US$ billions)*	3.4	1,022	988
Average annual growth, 1993-99			
Population *(%)*	0.0	0.1	1.9
Labor force *(%)*	0.0	0.6	2.3
Most recent estimate (latest year available, 1993-99)			
Poverty *(% of population below national poverty line)*	11	..	..
Urban population *(% of total population)*	60	67	31
Life expectancy at birth *(years)*	73	69	60
Infant mortality *(per 1,000 live births)*	15	22	77
Child malnutrition *(% of children under 5)*	..	8	43
Access to improved water source *(% of population)*	..	..	64
Illiteracy *(% of population age 15+)*	..	3	39
Gross primary enrollment *(% of school-age population)*	88	100	96
Male	89	101	102
Female	88	99	86

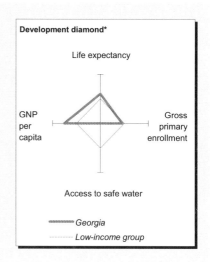

Development diamond*

Georgia
Low-income group

KEY ECONOMIC RATIOS and LONG-TERM TRENDS

	1979	1989	1998	1999
GDP *(US$ billions)*	..	..	3.5	2.7
Gross domestic investment/GDP	..	28.0	17.2	16.8
Exports of goods and services/GDP	..	42.4	20.9	27.0
Gross domestic savings/GDP	..	25.3	-3.6	-2.2
Gross national savings/GDP	..	..	5.9	8.8
Current account balance/GDP	..	..	-11.3	-8.0
Interest payments/GDP	..	..	1.1	1.2
Total debt/GDP	..	..	48.5	63.8
Total debt service/exports	..	..	7.2	11.9
Present value of debt/GDP	..	..	36.9	49.2
Present value of debt/exports	..	..	199.7	194.8

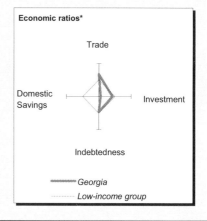

Economic ratios*

Georgia
Low-income group

	1979-89	1989-99	1998	1999	1999-03
(average annual growth)					
GDP	1.9	-17.2	2.9	3.3	4.8
GNP per capita	1.1	-15.9	2.2	4.1	4.8
Exports of goods and services	..	9.9	3.5	-1.5	8.0

STRUCTURE of the ECONOMY

	1979	1989	1998	1999
(% of GDP)				
Agriculture	..	23.3	35.6	36.0
Industry	..	38.7	13.0	12.9
Manufacturing	..	27.1	7.6	7.6
Services	..	38.0	51.5	51.1
Private consumption	..	62.6	90.2	89.8
General government consumption	..	12.1	13.4	12.4
Imports of goods and services	..	45.1	41.6	46.0

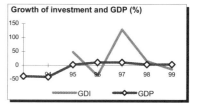

Growth of investment and GDP (%)

GDI   GDP

	1979-89	1989-99	1998	1999
(average annual growth)				
Agriculture	..	3.0	-8.0	3.0
Industry	..	5.1	-2.0	2.0
Manufacturing	..	3.3	-1.0	3.0
Services	..	19.0	16.5	1.7
Private consumption	..	6.8	9.1	-5.2
General government consumption	..	17.3	6.2	-11.4
Gross domestic investment	..	18.9	15.5	-14.4
Imports of goods and services	..	12.1	12.2	-12.7
Gross national product	1.9	-15.9	2.4	4.2

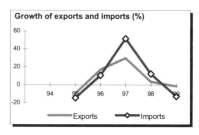

Growth of exports and imports (%)

Exports   Imports

Note: 1999 data are preliminary estimates.

* The diamonds show four key indicators in the country (in bold) compared with its income-group average. If data are missing, the diamond will be incomplete.

Table 1 (Cont.)

Georgia

PRICES and GOVERNMENT FINANCE

	1979	1989	1998	1999
Domestic prices				
(% change)				
Consumer prices	..	..	3.6	19.1
Implicit GDP deflator	2.8	5.4	4.5	9.4
Government finance				
(% of GDP, includes current grants)				
Current revenue	..	29.1	16.2	15.9
Current budget balance	..	29.1	-4.4	-5.1
Overall surplus/deficit	..	29.1	-6.4	-6.9

Inflation (%)

TRADE

	1979	1989	1998	1999
(US$ millions)				
Total exports (fob)	..	6,716	478	477
Black metal	..	..	39	33
Tea	..	..	43	39
Manufactures	..	..	222	249
Total imports (cif)	..	7,150	1,164	1,013
Food	..	1,685	325	281
Fuel and energy	..	481	205	187
Capital goods	..	1,710	231	187
Export price index (1995=100)	..	..	90	93
Import price index (1995=100)	..	..	95	95
Terms of trade (1995=100)	..	..	94	97

Export and import levels (US$ mill.)

BALANCE of PAYMENTS

	1979	1989	1998	1999
(US$ millions)				
Exports of goods and services	..	..	720	739
Imports of goods and services	..	..	1,437	1,260
Resource balance	..	..	-717	-521
Net income	..	..	117	119
Net current transfers	..	..	211	182
Current account balance	..	..	-389	-220
Financing items (net)	..	..	298	209
Changes in net reserves	..	..	91	11
Memo:				
Reserves including gold (US$ millions)	..	..	119	133
Conversion rate (DEC, local/US$)	..	..	1.4	2.0

Current account balance to GDP (%)

EXTERNAL DEBT and RESOURCE FLOWS

	1979	1989	1998	1999
(US$ millions)				
Total debt outstanding and disbursed	..	..	1,674	1,747
IBRD	..	..	0	0
IDA	..	..	274	346
Total debt service	..	..	66	113
IBRD	..	..	0	0
IDA	..	..	2	3
Composition of net resource flows				
Official grants	..	..	54	68
Official creditors	..	..	96	71
Private creditors	..	..	0	17
Foreign direct investment	..	..	50	62
Portfolio equity	..	..	0	0
World Bank program				
Commitments	..	..	27	115
Disbursements	..	..	53	79
Principal repayments	..	..	0	0
Net flows	..	..	53	79
Interest payments	..	..	2	3
Net transfers	..	..	51	76

Composition of 1999 debt (US$ mill.)

A - IBRD
B - IDA D - Other multilateral
C - IMF

E - Bilateral
F - Private
G - Short-term

Development Economics

Source: The State Department of Statistics

Table 2
Selected Socio-Economic Indicators for Georgia

	1989	*1990*	*1991*	*1992*	*1993*	*1994*	*1995*	*1996*
Crude Birth Rate (per 1,000 population)	16.7	17.0	16.6	14.9	12.6	10.7	10.9	11.1
Crude Death Rate (per 1,000 population)	8.6	8.4	8.7	9.6	10.0	9.4	8.1	7.1
Population Size (in 1,000s)	5 443	5 456	5 464	5 463	5 447	5 434	5 418	5 416
Net External Migration (in 1,000s)	-28.9	-39.0	-44.0	-41.6	-26.3	-31.5	-20.2	-11.7
Crude Marriage Rate (per 1,000 population)	7.0	6.7	7.1	5.5	4.9	4.5	4.4	4.0
Crude Divorce Rate (per 1,000 population)	1.4	1.4	1.4	1.0	0.7	0.6	0.6	0.5
Total Fertility Rate (children per woman)	2.14	2.21	2.15	1.79	1.64	1.66	1.71	1.69
Abortion Rate (per 100 live births)	76	66	67	66	73	85	77	60
GDP in 1990-1996 (in mill. Lari)		14.9	19.1	138.0	27.5	1 419	3 693	5 300
Real GDP Growth Rates (annual change)	-4.8	-15.0	-20.1	-39.7	-29.3	-12.1	3.3	11.0
Growth Rate of Industrial Production (annual change %)	-6.9	-29.9	-22.6	-45.8	-26.6	-39.7	-9.6	7.0
Budget Deficit/GDP Ratio (%)			-3.0	-28.0	-34.0		-4.7	-5.6
Annual Inflation Rate (%)	6.4	3.3	75.3	746.4	1037.2	7741.5	57.4	13.5
Total Consumer Price Index (%)		103.3	175.3	846.4	1137.2	7841.5	158.8	113.5
Food and Non-alcoholic Beverages (%)		108.7	186.8	1 118	15 141		153.8	108.1
Public Revenue/GDP Ratio (%)	31.6	33.3	29.8	10.2	9.7	7.7	7.7	9.8
Public Expenditure/GDP Ratio (%)	30.6	32.0	31.7	35.6	33.3	23.5	11.1	17.0
Budget Social Expenditure/GDP Ratio (%)							5.6	3.2
Budget Expenditure on Health/GDP Ratio (%)	2.9	3.2	4.2	2.8	0.4		1.0	0.3
Budget Expenditure on Education/GDP Ratio (%)	6.2	7.2	7.0	3.1	0.6		1.3	0.4
Family and Maternity Allowances/GDP Ratio (%)	0.5	0.6	1.8	1.3	0.2		0.1	0.1
Public Expenditure on Pensions/GDP Ratio (%)	4.5	4.8	7.9	5.6	1.3		1.8	1.5
Employment Rate (as % of working-age population)	84.3	87.0	79.7	63.2	62.8		61.8	
Annual Registered Unemployment Rate (%)			0.2	2.3	6.1	3.7	3.5	6.5
Minimum Wage/Average Wage Ratio (%)	35.6	31.0	41.4	36.8	26.6		25.5	23.6
Index of Per Capita Real Income (%)	109.1	100.0	79.2	77.2				
Food Share (% of consumption expend-s spent on food)	38.2	35.6	46.8	62.6	65.1	70.0	70.0	63.6
Area of Agricultural lands Under Cultivation (Thousand ha)		11 273	11 286	11 295	11 217	11 176	10 663	10 657
Immunisation Rate (% of children aged 1-2) DT	31.1	36.2	30.4	0.5	24.4	30.0	47.1	79.5
Polio	36.6	38.8	32.5	36.7	38.5	36.7	58.9	30.2
Measles	34.8	37.1	28.5	9.1	36.6	26.5	32.2	29.1
Infant Mortality Rate (per 1000 live births)	19.6	15.8	13.7	12.4	18.3	25.2	17.8	17.4
Total Number of Maternal Deaths	50.0	19.0	9.0	4.0		1.0	19.0	10.0
Number of Low Birth Rate Newborns (<2,501 grams)	585.0	757.0	506.0	387.0	736.0	421.0	339.0	538.0
Total Crime Rate (per 100,000 population)	324.0	361.0	402.0	443.0	406.0	325.6	255.0	

Source: The State Department of Statistics

Table 3
Main Socio-Economic Indicators of Georgia

	1997	1997 as % of 1996	December 1997 as % of December 1996
Gross Domestic Production, million GEL	6 431.0	111.3	...
Industrial production, million GEL	801.3	108.1	110.8
Capital Investments, million GEL	167.4	178.7	590
of which construction-installations works	75.6	157	800
Main funds functioning, million GEL	60.5	-	-
Dwellings completed, total floor space, 1000 m².	14.8	44.3	22.1
Agricultural production, billion GEL	2.5	109.5	X
Transport freight traffic, million tonne/km	5 973.5	80.1	690
of which railway freight traffic	1 955	171.3	132.4
Total retail trade turnover, million GEL	993.8	127.5	122.9
Services, million GEL	279.1	152.1	197.3
External trade,** million US$	1 108.7	134.1	111.6
of which:			
Export	250.1	125.8	123.6
Import	858.6	136.7	107.9
Average monthly salary of economy employees, GEL	54.9	189.7	167.5
Registered unemployment,*** thousand people	142.9	X	246.8
Consumer price indices	X	107.1	107.3

Note: * without individual building construction; ** ratio data are calculated at acting prices; *** to the end of period
Source: The State Department of Statistics

Annex C. Data of Forest Fund

Table 1

General Data of Georgian Forest Fund

	1995	*1999*
Total area of forest fund, (1,000.ha)	2 991.4	3 006.4
With forest cover, (1,000.ha)	2 760.6	2 773.4
% of forest cover	39.7	39.9
Total growing stock, (million m^3)	434.81	451.7

Source: State Forestry Department, 2000

Table 2

Forest Distribution by Managing Agency

	1995	*1999*
State Department of Forestry		
Total area 1,000 ha	**2 235.5**	**2 528**
Wooded 1,000 ha	2050	2 339.5
Growing stock million m^3	360.42	394.4
Institute of Mountain Forestry		
Total area 1,000 ha	**54.7**	**54.7**
Wooded 1,000 ha	43.4	43.4
Growing stock million m^3	4.6	4.6
State Department of Reserves, Protected Areas and Hunting Management		
Total area 1,000 ha	**181.3**	**181.3**
Wooded 1,000 ha	147.3	148.1
Growing stock million m^3	31.53	31.53
Forests of former collective and State firms		
Total area 1,000 ha	**519.9**	**242.4**
Wooded 1,000 ha	519.9	242.4
Growing stock million m^3	38.26	

Source: State Forestry Department, 2000

Table 3
Forest Distribution According to the Protective Categories
(1,000 ha)

	1995	*1999*
Reserves	169	169
Valuable wood massifs	4.7	4.7
Green zone forests	265.7	276.5
Close resort forests	115	119.4
Farther resort forests	775.5	923.6
Soil Protective and Water regulative forests	1 626.5	1 465.7
Protective-exploitative and valley forests	35	35.1

Source: State Forestry Department, 2000

Table 4
Forest Distribution According to Altitude
(% of total)

Altitude	%
0-1000m	2.3
101-250m	1.6
251-500m	3.4
501-750m	6.4
751-1000m	13.1
1001-1250m	16.8
1251-1500m	18.7
1501-1750m	17.8
1751-2000m	12.9
2001- up	7.0

Source: State Forestry Department, 2000

Table 5
Forest Distribution According to Slope
(% of total)

Slope (degrees)	*Total*	*Coniferous*	*Hardwood*
1 up to 10	5.5	1.6	2.2
11 up to 20	16.6	8.9	15.1
21 up to 25	16.6	14.8	18.9
25 up to 30	18.2	24.3	21.3
31 up to 35	19.6	27.5	23.4
36 up to 40	15.2	20.9	17.6
41 and more	8.4	2.1	1.5
total	100	100	100

Source: State Forestry Department, 2000

Table 6
Forest Distribution According to the Density
(%)

	Crown cover density							
	0.3-0.4	*0.5*	*0.6*	*0.7*	*0.8*	*0.9-10*	*Total*	*Average density*
Total	17.5	36.7	31.2	11.2	3.0	0.4	100%	0.54
Of which…								
Coniferous	18.6	35.1	31.6	11.5	2.8	0.4	100%	0.54
Broad leaf Hardwood	16.6	37.3	31.9	12.9	0.9	0.4	100%	0.54
Broad leaf Softwood	21.6	36.5	26.8	12.0	2.7	0.4	100%	0.54
Other species	18.9	34.6	28.9	12.6	4.0	1.0	100%	0.55

Source: State Forestry Department, 2000

Annex D. Wood Utilization

Table 1
Wood Production, 1940-1995

Product	*Unit*	*Year*							
		1940	*1965*	*1970*	*1975*	*1980*	*1985*	*1990*	*1995*
Industrial wood imports	1,000 m³ (sob)	323	557	408	345	318	347	190	24.9
Sawn wood		258	633	659	577	489	545	541	5
Veneer		2.5	5.1	5.7	7.4	7.3	7.1	6.5	0
Wood boards		-	-	4.2	7.0	21.8	22.7	4.2	0
Furniture	Million Rubles*	-	-	35.7	65.0	103.2	140.3	137.1	1.12
Pulp	1,000 tons	7.1	-	19.7	16.3	18.2	18.0	0	0
Paper		9.7	32.2	35.5	32.6	38.8	40.0	28.1	0
Cardboard		-	6.3	11.1	65.8	55.7	59.3	37.9	1.3
Parquet	1,000 m2	-	-	883.7	-	760	875	432	31

Note: *1988 prices.
Source: State Forestry Department, 2000

Table 2

Wood Products, production in 1997-2001

(1,000 m³)

	1997	1998	1999	2000	2001
Fiberboard	0			7.0	8.0
Sawn wood	1 500	10.0	15.0	25.0	
Plywood	0.5			1.1	2.2
Veneer	60.0			80.0	150.0
Paperboard	1.3			3.0	3.5
Paper	0			15.0	2.0
Board (semi-finished products)	0.5	2.5	3.2	4.5	6.5

Source: State Forestry Department, 2000

Annex E. Actual and Planned Forestry Activities

Table 1

Dynamics and Forecast of Wood Harvesting in Georgia

(1,000 m³)

1997		1998		1999		2000		2001		2002		2003		2004		2005		Total 1998-2005	
Final	Thinning	Final	Thinning	Final	Thinning	Final	Thinning	Final	Thinning	Final	Thinning	Final	Thinning	Final	Thinning	Final	Thinning	Final	Thinning
220	300	250	300	300	300	350	305	400	310	460	315	530	320	600	325	670	330	3 780	2 805

Source: State Forestry Department, 2000

Table 2

Dynamics and Forecast of Forest Road Constructions in Georgia

(km of road constructed)

1997	1998	1999	2000	*2001	*2002	*2003	*2004	*2005	Total
160	170	180	190	200	210	220	230	240	1 640

Note: *Forecasted

Source: State Forestry Department, 2000

Table 3
Dynamics of Reforestation Activities and Expenditure

	1998	*1999*	*2000*	*2001*	*2002*	*2003*	*2004*	*2005*	*Total*
Hectares	1 400	1 600	2 000	2 200	2 400	2 600	2 800	3 000	18 000
1,000 GEL	1 538.1	1 752.6	2 127.1	2 287.3	2 467.9	2 650.6	2 830.3	3 022.1	18 676.0

Source: State Forestry Department, 2000

Annex F. Non-wood Products

Table 1
Annual Yield of Edible Mushrooms in Georgia by Forest Type

Forest type	*Forest Area (1,000 ha)*	*Area of forest with mushroom growth (1,000 ha.)*	*Annual Stock on Total Area (tons)*		
			Minimum	*Medium*	*Maximum*
Oak and variations	220.9	17	170	300	800
Beech	1 051.4	80	800	1 600	4 000
Pine	102.3	10	100	200	500
Spruce fir	307.4	30	300	600	1,500
Total	1 682.0	137	1 370	2 700	6 800

Source: State Forestry Department, 2000

Table 2
Amounts of Medicinal Plants Harvested (green mass) and their Market Prices in Georgia.

Species	*Harvestable (tons)*	*Harvested (tons)*	*Market price (Lari/kg)*	*Roadside price (Lari/kg)*	*Collectors' revenue (1,000 Lari)*	*Estimated unit cost of extraction (Lari/kg)*	*Total cost of extraction (1,000 Lari)*	*Producer Surplus (1,000 Lari)*
Rosa canina L.	300	36	1.00	0.80	28.8	0.2	7.2	21.6
Sambucus higrum L.	300	36	0.60	0.50	18	0.13	4.68	13.32
Crataegus sangvineaps	200	24	0.50	0.45	10.8	0.11	2.64	8.16
Mentha arvensis L.	100	12	0.50	0.45	5.4	0.11	1.32	4.08
Urtica dioica L.	100	12	0.30	0.25	3	0.06	0.72	2.28
Plantago Moior L.	100	12	0.40	0.35	4.2	0.09	1.08	3.12
Rhododendron cerucasicum Pall	800	96	0.80	0.70	67.2	0.18	17.28	49.92
Pyrus camminis L.	300	36	0.40	0.30	10.8	0.08	2.88	7.92
Malus silvestris Mill	200	24	0.40	0.30	7.2	0.08	1.92	5.28
Hippophae rhamnoides L.	150	18	1.00	0.80	14.4	0.2	3.6	10.8
Senecio rombifolus	4 000	480	0.10	0.08	38.4	0.02	9.6	28.8
Chelidonium majus	100	12	0.60	0.50	6	0.13	1.56	4.44
Total	6 650	798						159.72

Source: State Forestry Department, 2000

Table 3
Annual Stock, Harvest and Collectors' Producer Surplus on Nut Species in Georgia.

Species	Chestnut	Walnut	Hazelnut	Cornel (Cornus Mas)	Total
Total Area (1,000 ha)	104.7	1.1	2.5	0.1	
Annual Biological Productivity (kg/ha)	200	100	50	100	
Annual Total Biological Stock (tons)	21 000	100	1 250	100	22 450
Annually Harvested Amount (tons)	4 200	50	150	20	4 420
Market Price (Lari/kg)	1	2	2	1	
Estimated roadside price (Lari/kg)	0.5	1	1	0.5	
Collectors' revenues at roadside (1,000Lari)	2 100	50	150	10	2 310
Cost of Extraction (Lari)	1 050	25	75	5	
Collectors' CS (1,000 Lari)	1 050	25	75	5	1 155

Source: State Forestry Department, 2000

Table 4
Population and Density of Game Animals According to the 1987-88 Inventory

Species	Population	Density (per 1,000 ha)
bear	6 000	3
boar	5 000	3
deer	1 100	0.7
roe deer	12 000	6
wolf	3 000	1
fox	26 000	9
hare	34 000	12
squirrel	40 000	20
marten	22 000	11
muskrat	65	
duck	6 000	
partridge	14 000	35
grey partridge	5 000	5
black grouse	12 000	20

Source: State Forestry Department, 2000

Table 5
Average Population and Harvest of Game Populations from 1967-71.

Year	Boar		Caucasian tur (ibex)		Roe deer	
	Population	Harvest	Population	Harvest	Population	Harvest
1967	7 000	40	10 100	23	10 000	78
1968	5 000	60	7 200	64	7 000	120
1969	7 000	80	12 400	28	11 000	140
1970	6 000	70	11 900	26	9 500	130
1971	6 200	80	9 600	47	10 000	150

Source: State Forestry Department, 2000

Annex G. Import / Export

Table 1

Logging Cost Structure: State Forestry Department Estimates for an average Grade Export Quality Beech Log

# Cost item	Estimate, USD/ m³
1. Stumpage Tax	$15.36
2. Harvesting labour, cash net of taxes	$10.00
3. Transport to District Centre (or railroad)	$15.00
4. Transport from District centre to border	$15.00
5. Equipment depreciation	$6.00
6. Personal income tax 20% on Net labor	$2.00
7. Social Payment 31% on Gross	$3.72
8. Harvesting block allocation fee to SFD	$1.25
9. Forest road repair (for one-time access)	$15.00
Subtotal Net Cost	**$83.33**
10. Profit Tax 20% (on export value less net cost)	$7.33
11. Dividend Tax 10% (on all retained cash	$2.93
12. Export Value	**$120.00**

Source: State Forestry Department, 2000

Table 2
Total Timber Supply to Georgia, 1971-90,
(1,000 m³ roundwood)

Year	Planned deliveries	Actual deliveries	Difference	Implementation
1971	255.36	201.28	-54.08	79.0%
1975	217.20	197.90	-19.30	91.1%
1980	262.15	196.50	-65.60	75.0%
1985	252.00	211.60	-40.40	84.0%
1990	253.24	149.71	-103.53	59.1%

Source: Statistics Department, Tbilisi

Table 3
Export Volumes of Round Wood, Processed Wood and Paper

Product	Unit	Year				Country
		1980	*1985*	*1990*	*1995*	
Round wood	m^3	-	-	-	15 000	Turkey
Veneer	*1,000 m^2*	2 000	2 300		-	Russian Federation Central Asia
sawn beech wood	m^3	200	2 000	-	-	Russian Federation
writing paper	*Ton*	820	775	800	-	Russian Federation
card board	*Ton*	-	8 710	12 112	96	Russian Federation
Corrugated paper	*Ton*	3 060	27 810	35 930	172	Russian Federation
Corrugated boxes	*Ton*	18 570	27 735	22 908	141	Russian Federation
Wrapping paper	*Ton*	-	-	379	-	Russian Federation
Note books	*1,000 pcs.*	10 500	45 600	34 690	-	Russian Federation

Source: Statistics Department, Tbilisi

Table. 4
Georgia: Trade Balance for Forest Products in 1999

Product	Unit	Import		Export	
		Quantity	*($1,000)*	*Quantity*	*($1,000)*
Sawnwood		**3 026**	**325**	**17 373**	**3 276**
Wood –Based Panels		**5 319**	**1 259**	**441**	**181**
Veneer Sheets	m^3	0	0	441	181
Plywood		1 082	352	0	0
Particle Board		3 259	670	0	0
Fibreboard		978	237	0	0
Wood Pulp		**181**	**100**	**297**	**164**
Mechanical Wood Pulp		84	29	0	0
Chemical Wood pulp		55	40	297	164
Dissolving wood pulp	tons	42	31	0	0
Paper + Paperboard		**6 299**	**3 906**	**194**	**345**
Newsprint		1 786	814	0	0
Printing +writing paper		2 473	1 775	116	135
Other paper + Paperboard		2 040	1 317	178	210
Roundwood		**2 061**	**143**	**57 524**	**7 890**
Wood fuel	m^3	**0**	**0**	**1 096**	**46**
Wood Residues		**10**	**1**	**0**	**0**

Source: World Bank/UN/FAO data base

Table 5.

Wood Exports in Georgia in 1999 by Importing Country

Country	Logs Volume (m³)	Value ($)	Unit Value ($/m³)	Processed Wood Volume (m³)	Value ($)	Unit Value ($/m³)	Total Volume (m³)	Value ($)	Unit Value ($/m³)	Percentage (Volume)
Armenia				235	23 000	98	235	23 000	98	0
Austria	34	3 000	88				34	3 000	88	0
China	1 355	139 000	103	569	89 000	156	1 924	228 000	119	1
Cyprus	43	3 000	70	1 265	108 000	85	1 308	111 000	85	0
Egypt	62	5 000	81	801	43 000	54	863	48 000	56	0
France	163	15 000	92	186	14 000	75	349	29 000	83	0
Germany	175	22 000	126	190	53 000	279	365	75 000	205	0
Greece	571	58 000	102	76 440	215 000	3	77 011	273 000	4	24
India				88	17 000	194	88	17 000	194	0
Iran				624	46 000	74	624	46 000	74	0
Ireland				86	15 000	174	86	15 000	174	0
Israel	15	3 000	200	8 082	118 000	15	8 097	121 000	15	2
Italy	763	95 000	125	59	11 000	186	822	106 000	129	0
Netherlands	40	4 000	100				40	4 000	100	0
Russia				2 205	50 500	23	2 205	50 500	23	1
Saudi A.				338	30 000	89	338	30 000	89	0
Slovakia	214	15 000	70	275	25 000	91	489	40 000	82	0
Slovenia	248	17 000	69				248	17 000	69	0
Spain	121	14 000	116				121	14 000	116	0
Turkey	28 058	2 523 000	90	201 209	1 764 000	9	229 267	4 287 000	19	70
Ukraine	50	2 000	40	80	4 000	50	130	6 000	46	0
USA				2 391	1 013 000	424	2 391	1 013 000	424	1
Uzbekistan				60	13 000	217	60	13 000	217	0
Total	31 911	2 918 000	91	295 183	2 450 000	8	327 094	5 368 000	16	100

Note: Where only timber weight was given, it was converted to volume using a conversion factor of 1 m³ = 0.65 ton

Source: Statistics Department, Tbilisi

Table 6

1997-1999 Timber Exports from Georgia

Year	Logs (m³)	Fuel wood (m³)	Processed Wood (m³)	Total (m³)	Percentage Processed Wood
1997	52 100		25 200	77 300	33%
1998	40 900	1 200	9 500	51 600	18%
1999	34 360		21 062	55 422	38%

Source: Customs Department, Tbilisi

Table 7

Values of Current Forest Uses and Services

(US$)

Forest Benefit	Annual Net Value
Direct Use	
Timber	12 000 000
Mushrooms	1 500 000
Nuts	580 000
Berries and wild fruits	1 950 000
Medicinal plants	80 000
Seeds	440 000
Forage	3 750 000
Hunting and fishing	2 100 000
Tourism and recreation	2 250 000
Indirect Use Values	NA
Option Value	NA
Non-Use Values	NA
Total	24 750 000

Source: Total Economic Valuation of Georgian Forests

Table 8

Resolution of the Ministry of Economics, Industry and Trade on establishing the wood market price

(GEL/ m^3)

Woody species	Timber price
Group I – *Taxus baccata, Buxus, Juniperus, Zelkova, Juglans regia*	300
Group II – *Quercus, Fagus spp, Fraxinus, Ulmus, Acer, Tilia*	200
Group III – *Fagus spp., Carpinus, Robinia pseudoacacia, Platanus*	130
Group IV – *Pinus, Picea, Abies, Cedrus, Cupresus, Cryptomeria, Tuya*	100
Group V – Other woody species	70

Source: Ministry of Economics, Industry and Trade

Table 9

Table for Calculating Stumpage Taxes for Woody Species

(tax per m³ in % in relative with the market price)

Group of woody species	Distance class	Barked timber (diameter at small end)			Unbarked timber
		thick 25 cm and more	*average* 13 – 24 cm	*thin* 4-13 cm	
Group I - *Taxus baccata, Buxus, Juniperus, Zelkova, Juglans regia*	1	34	30	27	5
	2	30	27	24	4
	3	26	24	21	3
	4	22	21	18	2
Group II – *Quercus, Fagus spp., Fraxinus, Ulmus, Acer, Tilia*	1	30	26	23	5
	2	26	23	20	4
	3	22	20	17	3
	4	18	17	14	2
Group III – *Fagus spp., Carpinus, Robinia pseudoacacia, Platanus*	1	26	22	19	5
	2	22	19	16	4
	3	18	16	13	3
	4	14	13	10	2
Group IV – *Pinus, Picea, Abies, Cedrus, Cupresus, Cryptomeria, Thuya*	1	22	18	15	5
	2	18	15	12	4
	3	14	12	9	3
	4	10	9	6	2
Group V – Other woody species					1
	1	18	14	8	5
	2	14	11	5	4
	3	10	8	3	3
	4	6	5		2

Note: Distance class I is from 1to 10 km from the main road or the railway; class 2, 11 to 25 km; class 3, 26 to 40 km; class 4, 41 and more.

Source: State Department of Forestry

Annex H. Institutions

Organization Chart and Functions of the SFD

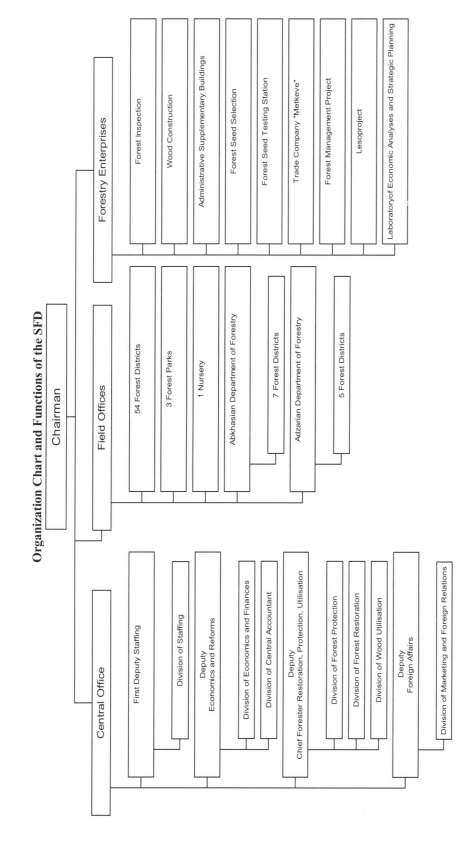

Chairman

Central Office
- First Deputy Staffing
- Division of Staffing
- Deputy Economics and Reforms
- Division of Economics and Finances
- Division of Central Accountant
- Deputy Chief Forester Restoration, Protection, Utilisation
- Division of Forest Protection
- Division of Forest Restoration
- Division of Wood Utilisation
- Deputy Foreign Affairs
- Division of Marketing and Foreign Relations

Field Offices
- 54 Forest Districts
- 3 Forest Parks
- 1 Nursery
- Abkhasian Department of Forestry
- 7 Forest Districts
- Adzarian Department of Forestry
- 5 Forest Districts

Forestry Enterprises
- Forest Inspection
- Wood Construction
- Administrative Supplementary Buildings
- Forest Seed Selection
- Forest Seed Testing Station
- Trade Company "Metkeve"
- Forest Management Project
- Lesoproject
- Laboratory of Economic Analyses and Strategic Planning

Administrative Structure of the Ministry of Environment of Georgia

Consulting Boards (Councils)

Minister and 4 Deputy Ministers

Secretariat of Minister

Functional Divisions

- Dept. of State Ecological Examination and Environmental Permitting
- Dept. of Protection of Mineral Resources and Mining
- Dept. of Biodiversity Protection
- Dept. of Water Resources Protection
- Dept. of Atmospheric Air Protection
- Dept. of Land Resources Protection, Waste and Chemical Substances Management

Central Office

- Dept. of Management and Supervision of Environmental Activities
- Dept. of Environmental Policy
- Dept. of Environmental Economy
- Legal Department
- Dept. of Human Resources
- Dept. of Finances and Planning
- Central Accountancy Dept.
- Chancellery
- Dept. of Purchasing

Subordinated Bodies

- Environmental Protection Institute
- Scientific Research Inst. of Marine Ecology & Fishery
- Environmental monitoring Centre
- Center of Reproduction of Rare and Endangered Species of Fish
- Coordinating Agency of Natural and Antropogenic Disasters
- West Georgia Complex Laboratory
- Adjara Regional Lab. on Environmental pollution Control

Double Subordinated Bodies

- Ministry of Environment of Adjara Autonomous Republic
- Ministry of Environment of Abkhazeti Autonomous Republic
- Tbilisi Committee of the Protection of Environment and Regulation of Natural Resources' Usage

Regional Bodies

- Khashuri Municipal Dept.
- Poti Municipal Dept.
- Samegrelo & Zemo Svaneti Reg. Dept.
- Guria Reg. Dept.
- Kvemo Kartli Reg.Dept.
- Imereti Reg. Dept.
- Shida Kartli Reg. Dept.
- Samtkhe_Javakheto Reg. Dept.
- Mtskhet-Mtianeto Reg. Dept.
- Kakheti Reg. Dept.
- Kvemo Svaneti Reg. Dept.
- Racha Reg. Dept.

Intergovernmental Licensing Councils

- Licensing Mineral Resources Usage
- Licensing of Surface Water Resources Usage
- Licensing of Flora Resources Usage
- Licensing of Fauna Resources Usage

Source: NEAP, 2000

State Department of Protected Areas

Chairman and 2
Vice Chairmen

Central office

| Division of State Reserves | Division of Wildlife (Fauna) | Division of Accountant | Chancellery |

Division of State Reserves

1. Lagodexi State Reserve
2. Vashlovani State Reserve
3. Axmeta State Reserve
4. Saguramo State Reserve
5. AlgeTi State Reserve
6. Borjomi State Reserve
7. Pitsunda-Miusera State Reserve
8. Ritsa State Reserve
9. Sataphlia State Reserve
10. Kintrishi State Reserve
11. Ajameti State Reserve
12. Gumusta State Reserve
13. Kazbegi State Reserve
14. Liaxvi State Reserve

Division of Wildlife (Fauna)

1. Borjomi-Xaragauli National park
2. Kolkheti National Park

1. 1.Korugy Habitat/Species Management Area
2. Iori Habitat/Species Management Area
3. Chachuni Habitat/Species Management Area
4. Katsoburi Habitat/Species Management Area

1. Aphazeti Division on Supervising of PA
2. Ajara Division on Supervising of PA
3. East Georgia Division on Supervising of PA
4. West Georgia Division on Supervising of PA

Some facts about the Timber Committee

The Timber Committee is a principal subsidiary body of the UNECE (United Nations Economic Commission for Europe) based in Geneva. It constitutes a forum for cooperation and consultation between member countries on forestry, forest industry and forest product matters. All countries of Europe; the former USSR; United States, of America, Canada and Israel are members of the UNECE and participate in its work.

The UNECE Timber Committee shall, within the context of sustainable development, provide member countries with the information and services needed for policy- and decision-making regarding their forest and forest industry sector ("the sector"), including the trade and use of forest products and, when appropriate, formulate recommendations addressed to member Governments and interested organizations. To this end, it shall:

1. With the active participation of member countries, undertake short-, medium- and long-term analyses of developments in, and having an impact on, the sector, including those offering possibilities for the facilitation of international trade and for enhancing the protection of the environment;
2. In support of these analyses, collect, store and disseminate statistics relating to the sector, and carry out activities to improve their quality and comparability;
3. Provide the framework for cooperation e.g. by organizing seminars, workshops and ad hoc meetings and setting up time-limited ad hoc groups, for the exchange of economic, environmental and technical information between governments and other institutions of member countries that is needed for the development and implementation of policies leading to the sustainable development of the sector and to the protection of the environment in their respective countries;
4. Carry out tasks identified by the UNECE or the Timber Committee as being of priority, including the facilitation of subregional cooperation and activities in support of the economies in transition of central and eastern Europe and of the countries of the region that are developing from an economic point of view;
5. It should also keep under review its structure and priorities and cooperate with other international and intergovernmental organizations active in the sector, and in particular with the FAO (Food and Agriculture Organization of the United Nations) and its European Forestry Commission and with the ILO (International Labour Organisation), in order to ensure complementarity and to avoid duplication, thereby optimizing the use of resources.

More information about the Committee's work may be obtained by writing to:

Timber Section
Trade Development and Timber Division
UN Economic Commission for Europe
Palais des Nations
CH - 1211 Geneva 10, Switzerland
Fax: + 41 22 917 0041
E-mail: info.timber@unece.org
http://www.unece.org/trade/timber

UNECE/FAO Publications

Timber Bulletin Volume LV (2002)   ECE/TIM/BULL/2002/...

1.   Forest Products Prices, 1998-2000

2.   Forest Products Statistics, 1997-2001 (database since 1964 on website)

3.   Forest Products Annual Market Review, 2001-2002

4.   Forest Fire Statistics, 1999-2001

5.   Forest Products Trade Flow Data, 1999-2000

6.   Forest Products Markets in 2002 and Prospects for 2003

Geneva Timber and Forest Study Papers

Forest policies and institutions of Europe, 1998-2000   ECE/TIM/SP/19

Forest and Forest Products Country Profile: Russian Federation   ECE/TIM/SP/18
(Country profiles also exist on Albania, Armenia, Belarus, Bulgaria, former Czech and
Slovak Federal Republic, Estonia, Hungary, Lithuania, Poland, Romania,
Republic of Moldova, Slovenia and Ukraine)

Forest resources of Europe, CIS, North America, Australia, Japan and New Zealand   ECE/TIM/SP/17

State of European forests and forestry, 1999   ECE/TIM/SP/16

Non-wood goods and services of the forest   ECE/TIM/SP/15

The above series of sales publications and subscriptions are available through United Nations Publications Offices as follows:

Orders from Africa, Europe and   Orders from North America, Latin America and the
the Middle East should be sent to: Caribbean, Asia and the Pacific should be sent to:

Sales and Marketing Section, Room C-113   Sales and Marketing Section, Room DC2-853
United Nations   United Nations
Palais des Nations   2 United Nations Plaza
CH - 1211 Geneva 10, Switzerland   New York, N.Y. 10017, United States, of America
Fax: + 41 22 917 0027   Fax: + 1 212 963 3489
E-mail: unpubli@unog.ch   E-mail: publications@un.org

Web site: http://www.un.org/Pubs/sales.htm

* * * * *

Geneva Timber and Forest Discussion Papers *(original language only)*

Forest certification update for the UNECE region, summer 2002	ECE/TIM/DP/25
Forecasts of economic growth in OECD and central and eastern European countries for the period 2000-2040	ECE/TIM/DP/24
Forest Certification update for the ECE Region, summer 2001	ECE/TIM/DP/23
Structural, Compositional and Functional Aspects of Forest Biodiversity in Europe	ECE/TIM/DP/22
Markets for secondary processed wood products, 1990-2000	ECE/TIM/DP/21
Forest certification update for the ECE Region, summer 2000	ECE/TIM/DP/20
Trade and environment issues in the forest and forest products sector	ECE/TIM/DP/19
Multiple use forestry	ECE/TIM/DP/18
Forest certification update for the ECE Region, summer 1999	ECE/TIM/DP/17
A summary of "The competitive climate for wood products and paper packaging: the factors causing substitution with emphasis on environmental promotions"	ECE/TIM/DP/16
Recycling, energy and market interactions	ECE/TIM/DP/15
The status of forest certification in the ECE region	ECE/TIM/DP/14
The role of women on forest properties in Haute-Savoie (France): Initial researches	ECE/TIM/DP/13
Interim report on the Implementation of Resolution H3 of the Helsinki Ministerial Conference on the protection of forests in Europe (Results of the second enquiry)	ECE/TIM/DP/12
Manual on acute forest damage	ECE/TIM/DP/7

International Forest Fire News *(two issues per year)*

Timber and Forest Information Series

Timber Committee Yearbook 2002	ECE/TIM/INF/9

The above series of publications may be requested free of charge through:

UNECE/FAO Timber Section

UNECE Trade Development and Timber Division

United Nations

Palais des Nations

CH - 1211 Geneva 10, Switzerland

Fax: + 41 22 917 0041

E-mail: info.timber@unece.org

Downloads are available at http://www.unece.org/trade/timber